Profane Justice

A Comprehensive Guide to Asserting Your Parental Rights

by

Suzanne Shell

Sage Wisdom PresS

Colorado Springs, Colorado

Bible verses quoted are from the King James Version unless otherwise noted.

Published by Sage Wisdom Press
PO Box 75863
Colorado Springs, CO 80970
(800)447-3081 ext. 7794

Printed in the United States of America

This book is dedicated to my beloved husband, Dennis. Who did right by my children. Who, when he was criminally charged with child abuse, did the righteous thing, even though it was the hardest and scariest thing to do. Who held me patiently and lovingly when I wept for him and for my children. Who stood staunchly with me to fight the corrupt child protection system. Who threw his unquestioning and wholehearted emotional, moral, and financial support behind me as I wrote this book without even knowing exactly what I was writing. If that isn't trust and devotion, I don't know what is. He is my hero.

ACKNOWLEDGMENTS

To my parents-in-law, who love me as their own daughter, and who believe in me.

I want to thank Scott Somerville and Michael Brown, who, in rare form, epitomize what a lawyer should be, for providing me with very valuable and complete legal information related to the issue of the child protection system.

I would also like to thank Mike Neligh who is the point man in the war against the fraudulent child protection system that pays a Federal bounty for our children, for sharing his unique information and putting me in touch with his knowledgeable contacts around the country.

Thanks, also, to Kelly Watt who provided me with bundles of stuff about the public schools.

Thank you to Mary Jane, Keane, who helped me tremendously with the U.S.C. 42 lawsuit details.

Special thanks to Linda Lowe, skillful proofreader, gentle critic and friend, and to Sandy Seifert, who also contributed her valuable proofreading and critique skills to polish off this project.

Finally, to all the families out there who bravely came forward to tell their stories, thank you and God bless us every one.

TABLE OF CONTENTS

DISCLAIMER

This book is not to be construed as advocating child abuse. True child abuse is abhorrent. It is not borne out of love and the desire to raise righteous and responsible children. It is an inappropriate expression of anger or a perverted act perpetrated on helpless children. Victims of such abuse need our help and protection. The full force of the law must be brought to bear against child abusers. Notice I said law. Child abuse is a crime, and it should be treated as such. Always. Social workers are not police, and therefore should not investigate child abuse crimes. Child abuse should be punished criminally, not plea bargained or tried in civil court.

The advice in this book is directed at non-abusive parents who find themselves facing the horrifying prospect of having their children unjustly taken away. Unfortunately, I must consider that the criminal abuser would desire to use the advice in this book to shield himself from justifiable prosecution. Therefore, this book has been prayerfully designed to frustrate any such attempt. Due to the very nature of criminal activity, they will not be able to accomplish the most important objectives found in this book, making this book useless in their endeavors to hide their criminal activity.

The information in this book is not intended to be nor should it be construed to be legal advice. Neither does the author represent herself as a lawyer. This is a book of public information and common sense. It is the result of five years of research into the child protection racket and the related laws. The author accepts no responsibility or liability for any action that occurs as a result of any person who follows or implements any of the information in this book. The reader is completely responsible for of his own actions and all subsequent results. The reader is strongly urged to conduct his own research and use his own judgement regarding all actions taken relative to this subject.

My intention is to present as many options as possible, along with the associated ramifications, and allow the reader to make his own decisions

The author also recommends that you seriously consider obtaining the services of a good lawyer to advise you concerning the law.

-Suzanne Shell

INTRODUCTION

Hosea 4:6 "My people are destroyed for lack of knowledge: because thou hast rejected knowledge, I will also reject thee. . ." KJV

The other day, as I stood at the checkout counter of a local discount store, I became aware of a young child screaming. Not crying. Screaming. The distraught mother tried to calm this little girl down by reasoning with her while she restrained her. When her attempts proved futile, she dragged the kicking and screaming child, who was about five or six years old, out to her car, which was parked near mine. I watched as this mother, who had barely concealed anger and embarrassment written all over her face, tried to get this recalcitrant child into the car. Each time she let go of the little girl's hand to unlock the car door, the child would run away, darting out into the parking lot. The mother had to chase her and drag her back.

Once the door was finally open, the girl refused to get in and the mother had to pick her up and place the kicking and hitting child into the front seat. She buckled the seat belt and closed the door, and the child commenced to violently kick at the dash and hit the window with her fists. As the mother tried to unlock the driver door, the child opened the passenger door and once again ran away. The mother chased this child three more times before she finally got into the driver seat.

As she backed the car out of her parking spot, the child opened the passenger door again! The child never stopped screaming and crying, and was audible even outside the closed up car as the mother drove away.

Besides being unbearably bratty, this child was placing herself and her mother in danger.

What was most astonishing to me about this incident was the age of the offending child. Such displays of temper usually appear around two years of age and can be effectively controlled in short order. Clearly, such controls were not employed on this child when they would have been most effective; at the onset of the behavior problem. The mother had no control over this child at six. I shudder what to think will happen at 13!

I wanted to approach this woman and give her my name and phone number. I wanted to tell her that she needed to spank this child and I would be a witness on her behalf if anyone turned her in for child abuse for administering the spanking. I didn't do it.

When my oldest son was a little over two, we lived in Berlin, Germany. He had begun having temper tantrums at home. At first, I isolated him in our hallway. It was empty, and he couldn't reach any of the door handles. I told him I didn't want to be around him when he behaved that way, so he could just be by himself. I quickly opened the door when he stopped having his tantrum and explained that I liked having him around when he behaved properly. He quickly grew bored having tantrums without an audience and began to employ more appropriate techniques of expressing his dissatisfaction.

Then he tried it when company was over, and I just did the same thing. He learned that such behavior was more embarrassing to him, because I still isolated him and someone else could see his shame.

Then he attempted a tantrum in a German department store. I calmly dragged him, kicking and screaming, into the ladies room. The walls around the toilet stalls in Germany go down to the floor, which in my opinion, was perfect for isolating him. I stuck him in one of the stalls, telling him that if he wanted to behave this way, he had to do it by himself, and held the door shut from the outside. You should have heard the German ladies fuss at me! I calmly ignored them, and within a few minutes, Jacob quieted down. I let him out and told him, "See, it doesn't matter where we are, I do not want to be around you when you behave that way." He *never had another temper tantrum, anywhere!* The entire process of training him not to have temper tantrums took less than six weeks.

What this demonstrates is that if you can resolve disobedient behavior while the child is young, spanking may not be necessary. The less you have to spank, the less likely you'll be to face child abuse charges.

You are probably asking, why do I tell you this anecdote, especially in a book that advocates spanking? It is to illustrate that, while spanking is appropriate, it does not have to be the *first* discipline technique employed. Other techniques, properly used and properly timed, can be effective, which could preclude the need to spank. I didn't need to spank Jacob when dealing with his temper tantrums at two and a half, but the six-year-old at the discount store clearly needed one. Spanking is just one tool of discipline, but it is the most controversial. It is tempting to get defensive and resort to spanking too soon, just to assert your parental rights, when something else could work. Just because those opposed to spanking present their position in an emotionally provoking way, does not mean you must succumb to their emotional manipulation by overreacting.

There are plenty of books written that detail the horrors and abuses against parents and families when someone is accused of child abuse just for administering a spanking, or for even less "offensive" forms of discipline. This isn't one of them.

There are plenty of books that tell you how to discipline your children, some excellent, and some very damaging and ineffective. This isn't one of them.

This book tells you how you can protect yourself against child abuse charges for disciplining your wilfully disobedient child, or for asserting your rights by home-schooling, or practicing your religion, or any other reasonable parental practice that you are entitled to.

If that fails, it helps you to prepare for and defend yourself against a false child abuse allegation. It is not intended as legal advice. I am not a lawyer. I am a parent who has faced the horror and expense inflicted by the system that is determined to prosecute righteous parents who, at the worst, merely spank their children. I made many mistakes during our child abuse investigation which cost me dearly. I wish I'd had this book so I wouldn't have made those mistakes, but it didn't exist anywhere, so I wrote it.

In order to stop this tyrannical invasion of our rights, we must stand on our principles and be prepared to fight aggressively for our rights. The social workers won't tell you what they are, and they won't protect your rights for you. Neither will the police nor the courts. They will casually violate your rights in their zeal to take your children. The most important thing you need to know is: If you don't know your rights, you don't have any rights. In order to fight for your rights, you must first know what your rights are. This book will provide that education, and tell you how to assert your parental rights.

TERMS

In this book I make reference to several generalized terms.

AGENTS OF THE STATE refers to social workers, prosecutors, police, judges, police psychologists, therapists, school teachers and counselors, and anyone else who receives their paycheck from THE STATE and works toward taking the custody of your children away from you.

THE STATE refers to any governmental entity or body politic that has or assumes valid or invalid statutory authority over you and your family.

SOCIAL SERVICES is a generic term that encompasses any STATE agency which intervenes with family matters, including Child Protective Services, Department of Social Services, Family Services, Human Services, and any other name or designation that refers to the same type of agency. These agencies are generally known for their penchant for filing civil lawsuits to obtain court-ordered intervention into allegedly abusive families.

TITLE 42 is a shorthand reference (for the purposes of this book only) to Title 42 of the United States Code (U.S.C.), sections 1986, 1985, & 1983.

CHAPTER 1

THE DESECRATION OF THE FAMILY

"Resistance to tyrants is obedience to God." Thomas Jefferson

There is a war raging over the control of our children. The cry of outrage is spreading across this nation, as increasing numbers of children are wrongfully ripped from their loving parent's arms and secreted away by the unscrupulous agents of the State. Many good parents are branded child abusers, and in their naivete, are abused and manipulated by a system that transcends any preconceived notion of injustice. Their trusting children are deceived and coerced into "disclosing" nonexistent abuse, unaware that they are being exploited by the very people who profess to protect them. Christian parents are especially at risk of prosecution.

"Not all child abusers are Christian and not all Christians are child abusers. But a surprisingly high number of cases of reported child abuse occur in Christian families."[1]

This quotation, by a domestic violence center director, Marie Fortune, is frightening, because many Christians employ the "rod of correction" on their

---

[1] Fortune, Marie. A commentary, Center for Prevention of Sexual and Domestic Violence, Seattle, WA. As quoted in A Manual for Clergy and Congregations by The Spiritual Dimension in Victim Services. David & Anne Delaplane

children, and spanking is considered by many so-called experts to be child abuse. This is often the only basis for removing children from the homes of loving, concerned, non-abusive parents who only want to raise righteous, responsible children. In spite of the fact that spanking is universally legal, false accusations of child abuse against parents who spank responsibly, abound. These families are routinely sacrificed on the unholy altar of the often childless "child savers" who care more for their jobs and their Federal funds, under the holier-than-thou guise of child advocacy, than the child they purport to protect.

A large percentage of these "child savers" claim to have been abused as children. Some actually have been abused. They cannot conceive of a normal, healthy family; of parents who discipline out of love rather than react abusively out of anger. They have made it their mission in life to protect all children from the abuse they suffered, whether those children need the protection or not.

Spanking is not the only excuse used by the system to take our children. There are documented cases of children being removed because a healthy mother breast-fed her baby, because a child suffered the common high-altitude affliction of a bloody nose, and because a mother properly rushed her child to the emergency room for accidentally ingesting Tylenol. Some of these cases actually involve the permanent termination of parental rights!

Everyone is at risk of illegal intervention. The criteria to be an abuser includes people who are reluctant to have the government run their lives, people who believe in corporal punishment (spanking), and people who are 'overly involved' in religion. These criteria affect a huge segment of our society, probably even you and your family. The time to act is before your family is victimized by this overzealous and corrupt system, because once they have your children, it's often too late.

Forewarned is forearmed.

Since I will be making references to my family's child abuse case throughout this book, I would like to share our story with you. We have already shared it briefly with the nation in November 1992 as part of a two-part report on the CBS Evening News with Dan Rather, Eye on America report on False Allegations of Child Abuse. Their report emphasized the emotional aspects of the featured stories and largely ignored the facts, and never even addressed the problems or solutions. My story will contain the facts. The rest of the book will present the problems and some possible solutions.

****

Jacob and Eric are my children by a previous marriage. Jacob was 13 and Eric was 10. I was married for eight years to my second husband, Dennis, who was a fair and loving stepfather to my boys. We have no children of our own. The boys had lived with us for about five of those eight years. For a long time, Dennis enjoyed a close bond with the boys. They even called him "Dad," even though he had never asked or expected them to. They felt, by their own admission, that Dennis was a better father than their real father. Our problems first arose when they mentioned this to their real father, who responded with immature jealousy and made the young boys (then eleven and eight) feel very guilty about these natural feelings. As a result, the relationship at home with their stepfather deteriorated rapidly. They no longer called him "Dad," and refused to do the things with him that they used to enjoy doing, like helping him do "guy things" around the house, and fishing and trail riding.

As time passed, Jacob, now 13, had become sullen, destructive, angry, and rebellious. Dennis and I encouraged him to express his feelings, but he refused. He had bought into the popular culture that parents don't understand teenagers; that today's teens are different from us than we were at that age. This alleged problem is contrived. I do remember being a teenager, so does my husband. We were acutely aware of what Jacob was experiencing, and we wanted to help him. We knew it didn't have to be as bad as society and the schools portrayed, and we had worked hard to establish good communications with him as he was growing up. I had always looked forward to the boys' teenage years. But unknown to us, he had been brainwashed by the schools, by television, by society, and by his real father who manipulated the boys' emotions in a manner typical of Parental Alienation Syndrome. In our confusion, and our desire to see he got help, we suggested he talk with his grandparents, or the pastor. He wouldn't respond when approached by them. Finally, to the point of desperation, we told him he had to talk to somebody, how about if he talked to the counselor at school? He said he would.

His behavior deteriorated. He became argumentative and deliberately disobedient, earning punishment upon punishment. We began to run out of ideas. Unknown to us, he began beating up on Eric. He lied. He was repeatedly suspended from school for fighting. He resented the fact that we wouldn't allow him to hang around with the 16-year-old neighborhood boys who had a history of drinking and driving recklessly. We later found out that he had been "coached" by the counselor at school, who told him, "If you don't like what your parents are doing, we can make them stop." As a result of this irresponsible statement, he began to provoke confrontations at home.

Meanwhile we tried all methods of discipline we could think of, short of spanking, to bring his behavior under control. We felt that thirteen was too old for a spanking. He was grounded. He had extra chores, etc. One day, while we confronted him about yet another incident of deliberately breaking the rules, he *yelled* at his stepfather. This earned him a spanking. The first one he had gotten in nearly a year. Dennis explained to him what he had done wrong by yelling at Dennis, and told him he would get eight swats. At this time, Jacob was as tall as I and weighed about one hundred pounds. I didn't feel eight swats were excessive given his age, his size, and his offense. He dropped his jeans, but his underwear stayed on, and Dennis administered the eight swats with a martinet.[2] This spanking was given without emotion or excessive force, just like all the spankings we administered. It was part of our clearly defined plan for discipline. I was in the room for the entire procedure, including the explanation. Frankly, if Dennis hadn't spanked him, I would have. He deserved it.

Since he had threatened to turn us in for child abuse on more than one occasion, I examined his bottom and found no bruising or strap marks; however, it was uniformly rosy!

Three days later, I came home from work to find a note from social services on the table. When I asked Jacob what it was he replied cockily, "Open it and find out." This attitude angered me and I resorted to a method I

---

[2]Pronounced mar-tin-ay. French. A wooden handle about ten inches long, with leather straps of the same length attached. Ours had the hard leather straps removed and replaced with soft suede. It has no mass, therefore it stings without causing injury.

often used when I was confronted with a situation I needed to think about for a moment; I told him to run some laps around the block. Instead, he ran over to a friend's house and called the sheriff, claiming I had kicked him out of the house and expressed fear for his safety, claiming I would beat him! He had never been beaten! But the school counselor had shown him how to push the right buttons to get his way.

The police came to my house and questioned me. Then they placed him in a foster home for four days to "protect" him. Eric was never removed from our home, and he was never interviewed by the police, social services, or the school counselor to corroborate Jacob's story. This kind of inconsistency, obvious to anyone with common sense, is often employed by the child savers. They have a pat answer for this, though, claiming the victim is a "'target child' . . . singled out for physical and verbal abuse."[3]

Initially, the investigator on the case claimed to have seen "three small bruises" on Jacob's buttocks, no less than three days after the spanking, where no bruising existed the day of the spanking. This raised the consideration of the bruising being self-inflicted, an imputation that was ridiculed by the prosecution as impossible, despite evidence to the contrary.

Later, during the trial, the investigator testified to seeing only a single small bruise. His description of either of the alleged bruising patterns did not match what the martinet could possibly produce, either in location or appearance. He claimed it was caused by the wooden handle of the martinet. Thank goodness I was in the room

---

[3]David & Anne Delaplane. The Spiritual Dimension in Victim Services. Page 44

during the spanking so I could verify that Jacob was never hit with the handle! No doctor or expert of any kind could verify any bruising. No photographs were taken.

While Jacob was in the foster home, we searched his room and found a homemade bomb. It was crudely built of plastic model parts and black powder, with a piece of yarn for a "fuse." While it wouldn't have exploded, we became concerned because of what it represented. We also found his pockets full of candy wrappers, which we learned could be an early sign of drug experimentation. Our investigation led us to suspect drug experimentation on the school bus.

Because of our discoveries, I informed the social worker that Jacob could not be unsupervised at any time, that he should not ride the school bus, and that she should not return him home to me on the appointed day until after six P.M. when I would be home. She ignored my demand and sent him home on the school bus, two hours before the time I told her. Eric, only ten, was faced with a decision a ten-year-old should never have to make, and locked Jacob out of the house. Jacob disappeared.

When I got home, Eric told me what happened. I was furious that Eric had been placed in that situation, and that Jacob was missing. I was unable to locate Jacob. The social worker showed up shortly and I confronted her about her foolish action of sending Jacob home unsupervised. I told her he was missing and she got scared and defensive. She stuttered and tried to assert control from the defensive position I had placed her in.

He showed up shortly thereafter, and the social worker became aggressive with me, attempting to assert her imagined dominance, demanding in front of the children that I refrain from spanking my children. I told her she had no legal ground to make such a demand, and to get out of my house. She was shocked that I wasn't intimidated or cowed. She repeated her demand, and I emphasized mine with an open door and pushed her out of my house, punctuating it by slamming the door shut. Then I loudly threw the dead bolt into the locked position.

That night I took Jacob up to an adolescent psychiatric hospital for evaluation and he was immediately admitted.

Drug testing revealed no illegal drugs in his system. Psychological testing revealed that he was experiencing violent fantasies, and was unable to distinguish fantasy from reality. The prosecutor wasn't interested in any of this important information that could prove valuable to Dennis' defense. In fact, she worked diligently, and successfully, to keep it out of evidence during the trial.

The doctor kept Jacob in residential care for several weeks. He was ultimately transferred to a long term residential care facility out of town. After nearly two years in and out of treatment, he was diagnosed with a seizure disorder that affected his ability to control his anger, and distorted his perceptions of what happens to him. This disorder was aggravated by the onset of puberty.

Meanwhile, the social worker kept contacting me, wanting to know where Jacob was. I told her he was out of the home, in a safe place, but I refused to divulge his location. To my reasoning, this should have satisfied their need to verify his safety, if that was their real concern. It wasn't. They wanted him in their custody.

While he was in residential care, the sheriff attempted to serve me and Jacob with a subpoena to appear in court. I dodged these attempts at service for over a week until I got Jacob out of state. His father had just moved to a new city in the southeast, and I sent Jacob to the Atlanta airport where his father picked him up. I instructed his father not to give me his address or phone number. Then I accepted service on the subpoena. They couldn't serve Jacob because they couldn't locate him.

When they couldn't locate Jacob, they served me with a subpoena to produce him. Since I honestly had no knowledge of his location, I didn't produce him on the pretrial hearing court date. The prosecutor asked the judge to cite me with contempt of court for failing to produce Jacob. The judge decided that if I didn't produce him on the date of the trial, she would make a ruling at that time.

On the date of the trial, the prosecution got a continuance. The trial was postponed because they still couldn't find Jacob. Throughout all of this, I refused to talk with Social Services or the police. Strangely, Dennis was never contacted by any of them, and he was the one charged with assault and child abuse! They wanted to harass me, and intimidate me into turning my son over to them.

They finally located Jacob the day before the new trial date. His school at his new home had sent a request for his previous school records and his new address was turned over the prosecutor by this school district. The prosecutor expected us to bear the cost of returning him to Colorado for the trial, and to house and feed him, while he was here to testify against his stepfather. But we knew that by law, if the state wants a witness to appear on their behalf, they must bear all associated costs, so we refused their demand to bring him back at our expense.

We had attended regular family counseling sessions with him for several months before he was transferred out of state. He never exhibited any remorse, and actually got worse in the care of the "professionals." He began to "own" the experiences the other teens shared during group therapy sessions. His stories became more outrageous. He began smoking and listening to rock music. Both were supposedly forbidden by the institution he was in. The therapy seemed to be doing more harm than good.

Because of this, I didn't want him to testify even though his testimony could only have helped us make our case because he constantly exhibited a defiant and rebellious attitude. I felt that if he were to testify, our lawyer would have to shred apart his testimony during cross-examination. In my opinion, this could have had a detrimental effect on his therapy as well as damaging him personally. I also didn't want him to witness the power the state attempted to wield against us as a result of his lies.

On the trial date, the judge ruled that I was not in contempt, because I couldn't be compelled to produce something if I didn't know its location. The only evidence presented by the prosecution was second and third-hand hearsay testimony and the martinet. I was forced to take the stand as a witness for the prosecution, because in a child abuse case in Colorado, a spouse can be compelled to testify against a spouse. Dennis also took the stand in his own defense. When the prosecuting attorney goaded him to anger, he devastated the prosection's case by reacting with control and reason, demonstrating proof that he did not strike out at Jacob in anger. The trial took two frightening days, and to our great relief, Dennis was quickly acquitted.

I wish this story had a happy ending, but it doesn't. This episode cost us thousands of dollars that we didn't have; it took us over a year to pay the lawyer. My children don't live with us anymore, either. I would not allow Jacob to live with us because I had promised him that if he falsely reported us for child abuse, he would not be allowed back in my home. I cannot allow a child to exert state control over my parental authority, so Jacob went to live with his father when he was released from residential care.

He was unable to have a good relationship with his stepmother, and he began to break all the family's rules. He constantly skipped school, and never finished ninth grade, the grade he was in when he last lived with me. He had some brushes with the law and ended up in juvenile prison twice. But while in prison, something good happened. He got his GED, and passed his ACT with a high score. Today, at eighteen, he has returned home and is now working toward getting his own apartment. He has since admitted that he went along with the story concocted by the counselor because it made him feel important, and it gave him some control over us.

Unfortunately, the boys' father believed the story of abuse, and refused to send Eric back to me after a Christmas visit a few years ago.

I never wanted to be a career woman. I have always wanted to have a large family. I loved having my children at home with me, especially while I home-schooled. I looked forward to watching them grow, and helping them become righteous men.

I have been through great physical trials to have my sons, almost losing both of them before they were born. I suffered four miscarriages while trying to have them and I cannot have more children.

My trials continued. My beloved sons no longer live with me, my family's bond having been broken by the corrupt child protection system. I also have borne a daughter, whom I reluctantly gave up for adoption when I was seventeen. The loss of my children tears at my soul with a profound sorrow that sometimes brings me to my knees in tears.

Rather than breaking me, these trials have made me strong. I have been called to use this strength to break the profane system that destroys God's righteous families and subverts parental authority over their children.

One thing you will learn from this book is that to fight the corrupt system, you must be strong. If you are the type of person who rolls over and subseviently licks the foot that kicks you when someone puts a little pressure on you, this book is not for you. If you cannot be strong, you cannot hope to win. I cannot stress it enough; it takes great courage and righteousness to face down such a corrupt, powerful and well-funded system. It may bankrupt you. It may tear your children out of your arms. This is a war, and there will be casualties, but you have more to lose by not fighting. If you ask for the strength, God will provide it.

CHAPTER 2

AN OUNCE OF PREVENTION

"An ounce of prevention is worth a pound of cure."
Benjamin Franklin

Before I had my first son, I spent much time and thought on how I would raise my children. I read everything I could find on the subject, especially pertaining to methods of discipline.

I had already been exposed to the argument that "hitting a child teaches him violence." The problem with this statement is the meaning of the word "violence." The liberal "child savers" have perverted the definition of violence to include such actions as shouting or yelling at someone, and slamming doors or throwing things that are not necessarily aimed at anyone. I disagree with this definition. So does the dictionary. Webster's defines violence as "use of physical force so as to damage or injure" and "an abusive use of force." Both sides of the spanking argument agree that violence is wrong. But when the child savers cite violence, they mean something entirely different than the rest of us do when we use that term.

While these expressions of anger may or may not be appropriate, they are not violence. I refuse to accept their perversion of the language to justify their claims. This perversion of the English language is pervasive today. It is very important that when you answer any questions for the agents of the state that you understand what the definitions of the words are. Otherwise, you may be admitting to something that isn't true. Make your questioners define the words before you answer anything.

You'll find that often you can answer honestly without incriminating yourself just by understanding exactly what they mean by their question.

This is the first line of defense against those who would take our children. We must insist on the accurate meaning of all words. By the actual definition, spanking is not violence. If they try to define spanking as violence, make them prove that definition.

My parents spanked me and I am not a violent person. I have committed no murders nor assaults on anyone.

According to a recent poll, 43% of parents spank their children. I question this figure. I believe that many more who do spank wouldn't admit it. To do so would expose them as being politically incorrect, and therefore "bad parents" according to the dictates of today's "experts" and often childless "child savers." Personally, I don't know anyone who *doesn't* spank their children. Even as I grew up, only one of my classmates claimed she never got spanked. In my years of working with others, I knew of one person who admitted she had never been spanked as a child. She was the only one who had no qualms about helping herself to my personal belongings in my desk drawers. She was unreliable, missing work often. This is how children who don't get disciplined turn out.

Even if only 43% of parents spank, and if spanking teaches violence, then *all* the affected children, or approximately 43% of the population, should be violent. Thus the "violence" argument breaks down when scrutinized.

I remember receiving spankings as a child. When I was very young, I was terrified of getting a spanking. Therefore, I did everything in my power to avoid one. It didn't always work, but the spankings I received had a profoundly positive impact on my attitude and behavior.

Fear can be a powerful motivator. This fear of punishment is not abuse, nor is a properly administered spanking. Both are effective training tools.

As I got older, spankings became more humiliating than painful. Sometimes, such humiliation can also be a positive motivating factor. I do remember, when given the choice of being grounded or spanked, I always chose the spanking because it was over more quickly. My children have consistently made the same choice given the opportunity. A punishment, swiftly and properly administered is not an abusive punishment, even in the eyes of the child being disciplined.

I also remember some spankings I got, as well as other punishments, that I knew I did not deserve. These made me angry and resentful. This is an important distinction, because "experts" claim that spankings cause anger and resentment. I disagree. Undeserved punishments, whether they are spankings or something less physical, cause anger and resentment. This can happen when parents take their frustrations out on their children in an unfair or excessive manner. They are being unfair and possibly abusive. Even the child recognizes this. This type of behavior is excellent fuel for the fire of family intervention.

HAVE A PLAN OF DISCIPLINE

The first way to protect yourself from child abuse charges is to have a clearly defined, *consistent* approach to discipline, one that is appropriate to the age and development of the child. Some experts recommend that this plan be written. This is necessary so that your children know what to expect for each situation, and so you have your guidelines to follow, too. This will eliminate any risk of your reacting in anger.

This approach can be very effective in convincing

a jury that you are a thoughtful and concerned parent who only wants to do the best for their children. It says you know what can be expected from your children at their level of development. In other words, you know their limitations, and that you tend to respond reasonably to their mistakes. It also portrays you as a parent who isn't parenting by accident but by a careful and prayerful design.

If you do spank your children, you will need to do it in such a way that they cannot dodge or squirm so as to cause unintended, possibly great, injury to themselves. A police investigator recently related the story of how a youngster tried to dodge his dad's belt. As he moved away from the position his father was expecting him to be in, his father accidentally struck him in his eye, destroying it. You can be sure that the father, in spite of his harmless intent and his anguish at his role in loss of his son's eye, was brought up on charges of child abuse.

You must also insure that the child does not attempt to protect his bottom with his hands. It is not your intention to strike the child's hands, so you must devise a way to protect their hands. This may require the help of someone else at first, but children can learn to keep their hands out of harm's way.

For a spanking, I made my children lean over a bed or dresser, with their hands supporting their upper body weight, and their legs spread away from the supporting object, somewhat like the typical position the police make suspects take when they want to search them. It is difficult for the child to quickly dodge into another position that might cause harm to them. You can be reasonably sure the only affected part of the child's body is the naturally well-padded bottom, eliminating the possibility of injury. There are other positions that can be equally safe. Whatever you decide, bear in mind that the child's safety is most important.

Discipline, especially spanking, should be reserved for **willful disobedience**. If you use the spanking for every minor infraction and accident, it will lose its effectiveness. If you must appear in court, your credibility will suffer if you confess under questioning that you routinely whack your children for every offense. People perceive spanking as a serious subject. It is best to reserve it for serious infractions of your rules.

I recently read a letter to the editor in the *Rocky Mountain News* from a prison inmate. He claimed that spanking was the reason he was in prison. Then he went on to say that his parents consistently spanked him for every minor or imagined infraction. He just eventually ignored the spankings, but the anger and resentment built up. This attitude carried over to his public life, and was reinforced by the ineffectiveness of the judicial system. Punishment is ineffectual, and means nothing to him. As far as he's concerned, he's a victim, first of his parents, and then of the system.

This "victim mentality" is reinforced by the liberal belief that nobody is responsible for their actions. It's always someone else's fault. You do not want to turn your children into "victims," you want them to be responsible. So you must be responsible with your discipline.

Sometimes our parents, who were our parenting teachers, used methods that were ineffective or reactionary. You don't have to be stuck in that mode. There are many books that address methods of discipline and the associated reasons for using them. I read many books in preparation for parenting, but I only used the methods outlined in two books; not surprisingly, by the same author. See the appendix for a list of recommended reading.

Along with a clearly defined approach to

discipline, you must also have a system in place for positive reinforcement, or simply put, rewards. Prosecutors will surely bring this up, and your confident and positive response will even further convince a judge or jury that you are not abusive. They will see you have considered the well-being of your children when you have a consistent system for acknowledging their accomplishments and rewarding their good behavior.

While I have made references to techniques that can help convince a jury of your worthiness as a parent, these techniques have the added benefit of reducing the chances you will even be charged with child abuse. While not being a guarantee of immunity from prosecution, you will be practicing a fair, effective, and reasonable approach to raising children. This obviously thoughtful and reasonable behavior on your part will weigh heavily in your favor against a rabid attack on your parental rights.

A word of warning: Never explain any of your parenting techniques to an investigating officer, police psychologist or social worker. The less said to any one of these people, the better it will be for you. It has been the nearly universal experience of parents who are accused of child abuse that whatever you tell investigators and social workers gets twisted and distorted into something completely different than what you said or meant. This distorted evidence will always be used against you in court.

The revelations during the O.J. Simpson trial regarding the perjury of police officers and investigators, and the tampering of evidence in the FBI crime labs came as no surprise to me. I have had close personal relationships with police professionals for more than eight years, and in my experience, they have all admitted, *to a man*, to lying on the stand and/or tampering with evidence to get a conviction. They justify this by saying that it is the only way to get the bad guys off of the streets. I think it also has a lot to do with being unable to admit they made a mistake when they charge an innocent person, as well as an abuse of their authority over someone they dislike for personal or professional reasons. Police aren't the only ones who perjure themselves. A San Diego County Grand Jury reports, "Attorneys, psychologists, and parents have all testified that some social workers lie routinely, even when under oath in court."[4] The less evidence you give them to distort or tamper with, the better for you.

In our child abuse trial, the investigating officer contradicted his own written report while under oath on the witness stand! The same goes for social workers. The "sworn" testimony of the school counselor in no way resembled what Jacob claimed he had said, but was horribly inflated to make us look as bad as possible. I cannot say if all officers are this way, but I would strongly advise talking to no one at all regarding what goes on in your home or in relation to any investigation involving yourself or your family.

In your fight to protect yourself and your family, you must not be an isolationist. Get involved with a church group or other organizations of high character, meet with other families regularly as a family. Child abusers are secretive. Therefore, you must bring your family out into the public eye. The families you interact with are able to develop a sense of your character and your family dynamics. They will know if you are a fair and reasonable parent or not. Their testimony can be invaluable in the event you need to put together a defense against false allegations of child abuse. This will also

---

[4]"Families in Crisis, Report No. 2" A Report by the 1991-92 San Diego County Grand Jury, February 6, 1992, pg. 21

prevent you from displaying any questionable isolationist characteristics that might be construed by the agents of the state to be a deviation from the norm.

THE STATE IS ACTIVELY TRYING TO DISCOURAGE CHURCHES FROM ADVOCATING CORPORAL PUNISHMENT

I attended a seminar sponsored by the County Victim Assistance (the Prosecutor's office), the Health and Human Services department (Social Services), and a Women's Crisis Center. It was entitled "Preventing Domestic Violence and Child Abuse: A Training for Ordained and Lay Spiritual Leaders and Christian Counselors."

This seminar was presented by "The Spiritual Dimension in Victim Services[5]." They proudly claim that they produced their manual under a grant from the U.S. Department of Justice. The State has placed its seal of approval on their interpretation of the Bible! This Denver-based organization presents this seminar all around the country.

I was concerned by what appeared to be the State attempting to influence what the churches teach, especially regarding corporal punishment. As this seminar progressed, I learned that my concerns were justified.

Their manual comes out strongly against spanking. "Professionals who daily must deal with child physical abuse uniformly speak of the fact that most physical abuse results from attempts to punish or control the child, which attempt has escalated to produce physical harm. For this reason, many are concerned when religions, in the basis of

---

[5] Rev. David and Anne Delaplane. The Spiritual Dimension In Victim Services. P.O. Box 6736, Denver, Colorado, 80206-0736. Fourth Edition.

the above quoted passages[6], advocate the use of the rod."[7]

They further assert, "There are many texts that would even seem to contradict the Proverbs texts, a primary example being Ephesians 6:4,

> 'Fathers, do not provoke your children to anger, but bring them up in the nurture and instruction of the Lord[8] [sic].'"

There is no notation in the manual of which translation this is.

To illustrate how they twist the meaning to match their desires, the King James Bible quotes this verse as,

> "And, ye fathers, provoke not your children to wrath: but bring them up in the nurture and admonition of the Lord."

The word "admonition" which means "rebuke," has been changed in the government sanctioned version to "instruction" which means "to teach." It seems that some people cannot bear even a simple, justified rebuke. It doesn't fit in with their notion of kinder and gentler, albeit ineffective, child raising.

But, for the sake of accuracy, let's look at the original meaning. The original Greek word, nouthesía, is explained as: training by word of encouragement when sufficient, but also by word of remonstrance, reproof, and/or blame as required. It also involves correction *by deed as needed* (emphasis added). There is attached to this

---

[6] The passages mentioned in the quote above include: Proverbs 13:24, 22:15, and 23:13,14.

[7] Rev. David and Anne Delaplane. The Spiritual Dimension In Victim Services, Fourth Edition. Page 43.

[8] Ibid

an appeal to reasonable faculties.[9]

Upon examination, their claim of a Biblical contradiction is clearly false. This verse does provide for more than just the use of words in bringing up children. But they cannot present this verse accurately and still support their position, so they must resort to deceit.

During the seminar, the various speakers employed as many emotional trigger phrases as they could to convince the attendees of their position. With a profoundly wise look on their faces, they said, "In this country, it's illegal to beat your wife, but it's OK to beat your kid." This is an overt lie. It is *not* legal to *beat* your kid. What they intentionally fail to point out is that there is a distinct difference between a beating and a spanking. They routinely use words like "beat" and "whip" to prejudice popular opinion against the more benign act of spanking, and to intimidate those who spank.

They also asked, "How would you feel if your boss hit you when you made a mistake?" This absurd correlation between an adult's mistake and a child's disobedience is patently ridiculous. But they are rarely if ever called on to support such an absurd premise. Part of the problem, too, is that they view children simply as small adults, endowed with adult rights and adult abilities. They do not acknowledge the fact that children cannot reason as adults do, cannot comprehend as adults do, and do not respond as adults do, and therefore cannot logically be treated as adults. They also believe children are innocent and inherently good. This belief is confuted by Proverbs 22:15, "Foolishness is bound in the heart of a child; but the rod of correction shall drive it far from

---

[9]The Hebrew Greek Key Study Bible, King James Version, AMG Publishers

him."

They also claim, categorically, that corporal punishment is "legalized child abuse." The intent here is to blur the distinction between spanking as discipline and beating, and to criminalize spanking.

"Child savers" are personally offended by spanking, which causes pain and humiliation. They make the claim that if corporal punishment is used as a training method, it is ineffective. According to their studies, learning is decreased by 80% when accompanied by pain and humiliation. They have overlooked one important word: punishment. Sometimes, as unpleasant as it may be, punishment is needful.

According to these "child savers," we should look to other "Biblical texts which speak of child rearing . . . (that) use more general, positive terms such as 'discipline,' 'nurture' and 'train up'"[10] to the exclusion of the offensive Proverbs texts. They do not view all biblical references to child raising to be equally valid in today's world. They treat the Bible like a smorgasbord, selecting those passages that they like, and discarding the passages that offend them. In their foolishness, they believe they are wiser and more compassionate than God, that this generation of man is more enlightened and civilized than previous generations. Therefore, we are no longer required to follow the outdated guidance given in the Holy Scriptures.

SUPREME COURT DECISIONS REGARDING PARENTAL RIGHTS

There are rulings that have clearly protected the rights of parents against intrusions by others, including by the state.

---

[10]Ibid

This is especially important, as in most cases the state objected to the way parents were raising their children. Today's popular battle cry is "save the children" and "Children First," regardless of the rights of the parents. This is taken to the extreme of violating the rights of parents and classifying spanking and other forms of parental restriction on a child's behavior as child abuse on the basis of personal preference rather than the letter and spirit of the law. So, what exactly are the rights of parents?

In *Meyer v. State of Nebraska*, 262 U.S. 390 (1923), the court decided that the Constitution limits the use of state power to undermine parental rights and undermine the family. "The liberty guaranteed by the 14th Amendment to the Federal Constitution denotes . . . the right of the individual . . . to marry, establish a home and bring up children, to worship God according to the dictates of his own conscience, and generally to enjoy those privileges long recognized at common law as essential to the orderly pursuit of happiness by free men."

Shortly after *Meyer*, another case was decided that stated that the parents have a substantive due process right to "bring up children." This case was *Pierce v. Society of Sisters, 268 U.S. 510 (1925),* and says "Under the doctrine of Meyer v. Nebraska . . . ,we think it entirely plain that the [1922 Oregon state law compelling public school attendance] unreasonably interferes with the liberty of parents and guardians to *direct the upbringing and education of children under their control*" (emphasis added). It also states, "The fundamental theory of liberty upon which all governments in the Union repose excludes any general power of the state to standardize its children by forcing them to accept instruction from public teachers only. This is not a mere child of the state; those who nurture him and direct his destiny have the right, coupled with the high duty, to recognize and prepare him for additional obligations." This decision held that the right of parents to raise their children without unreasonable state interferences is one of the unwritten liberties protected by the Due Process Clause of the Fourteenth Amendment.

In *Wisconsin v. Yoder, 406 U.S. 205 (1972)*, the court says " . . . the values of parental direction of the religious upbringing and education of their children in the early and formative years have a high place in our society."

"The history and culture of Western civilization reflect a strong tradition of parental concern for the nurture and upbringing of their children. This primary role of the parens in the upbringing of their children is now established beyond debate as an enduring American tradition."

Parents' rights to exercise their own best judgement in raising their children was further supported in *Prince v. Massachusetts, 321 U.S. 158 (1943).* "Constitutional interpretation has consistently recognized that the parents' claim to authority in their own household to direct the upbringing of their children is basic in the structure of our society. It is cardinal with us the custody, care and nurture of the child reside first in the parents, whose primary function and freedom include preparation for obligations the state can neither supply nor hinder."

Children are not the property of the state as stated in *Parham v. J.R., 442 U.S. 584 (1979),* "Our jurisprudence historically has reflected Western civilization concepts of the family as a unit with broad parental authority over minor children. Our cases have consistently followed that course; our constitutional system long ago rejected any notions that a child is the 'mere creature of the state' and, on the contrary, asserted that parents generally 'have the right coupled with the high duty, to recognize and prepare [their children] for additional obligations.'"

What is more important, *Parham* also makes a profound statement against the concepts held in the U.N. Convention on the Rights of the Child by stating, "The law's concept of the family rests on a presumption that parents possess what a child lacks in maturity, experience, and capacity for judgment required for making life's difficult decisions. More important, historically it has recognized that natural bonds of affection lead parents to act in the best interest of their children."

"That some parents may at times be working against the interests of their children . . . creates a basis of caution, but is hardly a reason to discard wholesale those pages of human experience that teach that parents generally do act in the child's best interest. The statist notions that governmental power should supersede parental authority in all cases because some parents abuse and neglect children is repugnant to American tradition."

"Simply because the decision of the parent is not agreeable to the child or because it involves risks does not automatically transfer the power to make that decision from the parents to some agency or officer of the state . . . Most children, even in adolescence, simply are not able to make sound judgements concerning many decisions, including their need for medical care or treatment. Parents can and must make those judgements."

The court's decisions notwithstanding, you still must take steps to protect your family. In practice, the department of social services doesn't care about court rulings or your rights.

DO'S AND DON'TS

These days we are constantly being told there are no absolutes and that right and wrong is relative. A look at today's headlines clearly shows where *that* has gotten us!

It could be said that the need to address the subject of being accused of child abuse for administering appropriate and effective discipline derives from this conflict of viewpoints on absolutes.

The potential for being accused of child abuse for disciplining your children can be vastly reduced by adhering to a few basic, but important principles. You will find that these principles are nothing new, but rather, are time-honored values that have a strong Biblical basis.

DIVORCE

I could say it all in one word: **DON'T!**

OK, but why not?

Recently a police investigator made an astonishing public comment. He said police rarely see child abuse and neglect cases in families who do everything together as a family. How eloquent. How simple. How true.

For decades now, we have been told by the "experts" that children can recover from divorce. They are resilient. They can adapt. History has proven these experts wrong, but most still refuse to admit it. This is because it doesn't fit in their "me first" style of marriage and they must be able to rationalize their selfishness.

Studies have proven that the best situation for children is for the parents to stay together. Second best is if *one of the parents dies.* How profound that such a tragedy is better for children than the parents getting divorced! Even a contentious home is better for a child than a divorce. The impact of divorce on children is profoundly negative, affecting their perceptions of themselves, their behavior, and their ability to develop healthy relationships throughout their lives.[11]

The world of the child revolves around his parents. Mothers and fathers serve different but equally important roles in the care and upbringing of the child. This bond cannot be harmlessly severed, even partially.

In a divorce situation, the child finds his loyalties divided, many times by the actions of the parents themselves. My parents divorced when I was in junior high school, and I couldn't bear to have one speak badly of the other, no matter how justified. I felt defensive and protective, yet torn with the love I felt for both of them. Ultimately, in an immature attempt to eliminate the conflict I suffered, I felt I had to make a choice between my parents. All children of divorced parents will eventually have to make a similar choice. This is not a choice that a child should have to make.

In even the friendliest of divorces, children learn to equivocate, instinctively knowing that their beloved mother and father are adversaries. This causes great pain for the child. Eventually, resentment builds up, and the child starts to act out.

This acting out, which can manifest itself in many forms of disobedient and oppositional behavior, can set your family up for child abuse charges based on your disciplinary actions to bring your child under control.

These children are more likely to abuse drugs and alcohol. They run away from home more frequently. They are more likely to become sexually promiscuous. They defy authority, at school and in the home, and act disrespectfully to adults. Put this, the worst of attitudes and behaviors, on the already heavily burdened shoulders

---

[11]L. Alan Sroufe, Ph.D. Professor, Institute of Child Development, University of Minnesota. 1989 Attachment Theory and the Aftermath of Divorce.

of a single parent, and you have a recipe for disaster. Add a stepparent and you have a prosecutor's dream.

I have listened to the stories of dozens of families who have been falsely charged with child abuse. An overwhelming number have one thing in common: A stepparent who was charged with child abuse. Stepparents are in a uniquely dangerous position with regard to child abuse charges. This is an incredible disaster, especially when you consider that a stepparent has married an entire family, not just a person. They have agreed to raise their spouse's children as their own, out of love. They didn't have to do that. And now, as a result of the overzealous prosecution of unfounded or false charges, their job, their finances, their very freedom is in jeopardy. This often sows the seeds of yet another divorce.

The danger is greater for stepparents because the state often claims that they don't have the bond with the child that the natural parents do, therefore, the instances of abuse in families with stepparents rises.

In a melded family, the natural parent finds herself torn between the children and the husband. This can be devastating when natural parents are forced to choose between their spouse and children. I personally handled this by informing all my guys, right from the beginning, that I would not make that decision. I told all of them that whoever gave me the ultimatum, "Either he goes or I go," had better be prepared to go himself. I felt that someone who forced me to make such a choice didn't love me very much, and therefore I couldn't choose him. During all of our struggles, no one ever demanded that I make that choice.

The process of divorce also puts parents in jeopardy of child abuse charges. If the custody of the children is contested, many times one parent will level child abuse allegations at the estranged spouse in order to have the custody issue resolved in their favor. And since, in a child abuse case, you are guilty until proven innocent, it is generally effective.

When a child's parents get divorced, the child will always have an out. When things get tough in one home, they always have in the back of their minds, no matter how outrageous it might be, that they can just go live with the other parent. Therefore, they have no commitment to solve their problems. They can run away from their problems and go live with Disneyland dad. And will dad refuse the child this escape, especially if the child hints at how abusive it is at mom's house? Of course not! Remember, mom and dad are adversaries. It is the rare child who will not learn to manipulate this to their advantage. Children who live in a home with both parents don't have this escape. They must face and solve their problems, no matter how difficult or unpleasant.

Your family can reduce its chances of experiencing these problems by refusing to consider divorce. Nobody wins in a divorce, but the children are the biggest losers of all, suffering on the altar of selfish adults who refuse to address and resolve their problems. And society doesn't help by making a divorce so easy to get, especially no-fault divorces.

What if the marriage is really bad? I know of one like that. The parents snipe and snarl at each other, getting in their digs at each other, even in front of the children. There is no intimacy, no respect, and little love. Yet as terrible as this marriage is, it is better for the children and the parents, than divorce. These parents adore their children, and heap love and attention on them. They are both there for them to share the good times and help them through the troubles. The husband and wife both have some needs met by the other. Divorce is not an option for this family. Neither is an adulterous relationship outside the marriage. Strange as it sounds in today's society, they will not consider either option. I can only pray that this small seed of wisdom will grow, and they can put aside their animosity and strive to have a healthy relationship with each other.

The issue of the abusive spouse must be addressed. If the abuse won't stop, if the abuser won't get help, the abuser belongs in prison. Nobody should endure abuse, not wives, not husbands, not children. As far as divorce, it's a tough call, and should be made with careful consideration. One thing is certain. Without help, the abuser will eventually abuse the children. Guaranteed. Often, children who see their mother being abused grow to hate the abusive father, and are greatly relieved when he is no longer there.

If marriage isn't easy, divorce is harder. I speak from experience. The entire family suffers, with some of these problems taking years to become manifest. It is easier to work through most marital problems than to allow even one of the parties to run away from them and bail out through divorce. All of the problems caused by divorce are 100% preventable.

It is hard to see this when you are on the inside, close to the issue. I was blind to the terrible effect my divorce had on my children. I have since had an opportunity to be closely involved with a teenager whose parents are breaking up, and I can see the devastating effects on his life, his attitude, and his outlook. He is somewhat embarrassed by his parents' breakup, and badly hurt. He often makes little comments, as if in passing and not important, about how he feels. He sometimes makes obviously painful, mildly denigrating remarks about his parents' absence in his life. He clearly feels abandoned, ignored, angry, and has demonstrated low self-esteem and lack of motivation. The money they throw at him to assuage their guilt is largely unappreciated. He doesn't want their money. He wants their love and attention. He wants his mom and dad. He wants his family. He needs his family. This is not an unreasonable desire for a child of any age. He has compensated for his loss by bonding with his employer to a degree that exceeds the employer-employee relationship. The employer has commented that he seems to be in an authority position that includes the parent's role as well as the boss's role. The boy seems to be a good kid, but he's terribly unhappy with his parent's behavior, and not unreasonably so for a child. This is only the beginning for him. His road will be harder because of his parents' divorce

You don't have the option of being selfish in a marriage, especially if you have children. You made a commitment, and you must stick with it, for the sake of everyone, especially the children. Yes, it is an old-fashioned concept. However, it has stood the test of time much better that the contemporary concept of casual commitments. At least for the children.

PUBLIC SCHOOL

"Every child in America who enters school at the age of five is mentally ill, because he comes to school with allegiance toward our elected officials, toward our founding fathers, toward our institutions, toward the preservation of this form of government, patriotism, nationalism sovereignty. . .All of that proves the children are sick, because the truly well individual is one who has rejected all of those things and is what I would call the true international child of the future." Dr. Pierce, Harvard University, 1973

The next most important action to take to reduce your chances of being falsely charged with child abuse is to remove your children from the public schools. All of them, all ages. "But," you say, "my child's school is excellent."

I'll make you a promise: If you keep your children in the public schools, all your attempts to protect yourself will probably be in vain. Police statistics indicate that the overwhelming number of reports of child abuse comes from the schools. The same schools that report the alleged abuse will surrender custody of your child without a qualm. They will cooperate fully in any investigation against you. Their words can bankrupt you, cost you your job, and destroy your family regardless of whether you win or lose your case.

When confronted by irate parents, the staff will claim that they did conduct an investigation before making the report. This is just a cover-up. They rarely, if ever, verify any statements made by the child, or accusations inferred by the staff member who interviewed the child. They never even corroborate the incident of alleged abuse with the siblings who might be in the same school. The only "investigation" they conduct is to question the child from the perspective of believing the abuse exists and make false assumptions. Often, administrators will admit they don't verify whether an allegation is accurate, or even if an allegation was actually made by the child or just imagined by the staff member. They report everything as suspected child abuse.

If that wasn't enough, the evidence clearly shows that you cannot fight six to eight hours of public school indoctrination and misinformation with an hour or two of quality time in the evening. With the passage of Goals 2000 and School to Work, coupled with the overt plans to invade family privacy and usurp parental authority under the guise of education and children's rights, the only protection you have is to remove your children from the system completely. It is too big and too overwhelming to protect your children from its pervasively destructive influence. If you won't remove them, then you might as well kiss all your rights, and your children, goodbye.

SCHOOL POLICIES ON REPORTING CHILD ABUSE

It is the law: all school administrators, teachers, and counselors must report suspected cases of child abuse. "'Reasonable suspicion' based on objective evidence is all that's needed to report."[12] This in and of itself is not a problem. It certainly makes sense that the institution that has such prolonged contact with children would be charged with protecting them from abuse.

But our public schools are heavily influenced by the National Education Association and the National Parent Teacher Association. These organizations are against fundamental Christian values, which they label as extreme.[13] This includes corporal punishment, the concept of absolute right and wrong, and parental authority. They also oppose home-schooling. These views are the basis for the persecution of parents who do not conform to their standards.

Basically, they abuse the law by "suspecting" child abuse when a parent rightly disciplines their child. The

---

[12]American Humane Association Fact Sheet #5. *What Should I Know About Reporting Child Abuse?*

[13]National PTA's Guide to Extremism. 9-93
1995 NEA Resolutions

child will be in some confusion because of the mixed messages he receives. The parents spank and the school says it is wrong. Naturally, because the child would love to get away with misbehavior, he will mention this spanking to a trusted adult at school. This teacher or counselor has specific guidelines to follow for this particular circumstance.

The staff is instructed to believe the child. Let me repeat that: The staff is instructed to *believe the child.* Unconditionally. They must calmly reassure and support the child with phrases like, "I'm glad you told me; you did the right thing[14]," and "It's not your fault," and "You're not alone, this happens to other children." With these phrases, the staff member becomes a defender of this child, and thereby creates an adversarial situation between the parent and the child.

Then they say something like, "I have to tell someone (a counselor or a police officer) that this has happened. They will want to ask you some questions. They can help to make sure you're safe," implying that the child is in danger. This can be an exciting power play for a disgruntled child. Sometimes they are further instructed not to ask leading questions or pry for details. This advice is rarely followed by school staff. There are numerous documented cases of school counselors playing amateur psychologist. They ask leading questions and imply answers that don't fit with the facts. The child is not aware he is being manipulated by these staff members to present the story the staff wants presented. If the child denies the implications of the questioner, the questioner will conveniently forget their admonition to "believe the

---

[14]The Frontenac County Board of Education. *Child Abuse: A Handbook for Staff.*

child," because it doesn't fit in with their imagined scenario. They'll insist the child recanted because he is afraid of his parents.

Another problem is that the child will simply say what the authority figure wants to hear in order to gain their approval, regardless of its accuracy. According to the 1991-92 San Diego County Grand Jury Report on Families in Crisis, " . . . sometimes children will lie and sometimes children will give a version of events they believe will please an authority figure."[15] They may make these statements based on the assurance that their parents will not get in trouble rather than out of an angry need for revenge. Children are generally trusting, especially of their teachers. This is clearly an abuse of that trust.

Often, when questioned about what they told the counselor, the child denies parts of the story as presented by the staff member. When my son, Jacob, was presented with the testimony of the school counselor, he denied that that was what he had told her. Yet, this hearsay was admitted into evidence during our trial!

Almost always, the staff member, or even the police will lie to the child in order to get more information. Such lies include claims that the parents will not get into trouble and that the child will not be removed from the home. But the children are often removed from the home, sometimes unwillingly, and the parents always get into trouble. These children are manipulated and victimized by a system that is more interested in dollars than protecting them or their families.

They are told they won't be held against their will, but when they want to return home, their requests are

---

[15]"Families in Crisis, Report No. 2; Recommendations" A Report by the 1991-92 San Diego County Grand Jury, February 6, 1992 pg. 48

refused.

The children are never told that if they are lying and making a false accusation, they can be charged criminally. This alone could make many kids who "cry wolf" back down.

They are given positive responses from the questioners every time they make their accusation, and receive disapproval or disinterest whenever they try to deny the allegations. This manipulates the children psychologically, who naturally seek approval from adults. They will recognize that the questioner is only interested in the nasty stuff, and will naively oblige.

As a result of this kind of investigation, the parents feel betrayed by their children, and their special bond and trust is badly damaged if not destroyed. It is incredibly difficult, if not impossible, to restore this trust. The family has effectively been split by the school, and the parents lose much of their ability to influence the upbringing of their children.

You're probably wondering: how do the children know to report spanking as abuse? They are being taught in the schools that spanking is wrong, that it is abuse. In my particular school district, social workers from the department of Social Services come into the schools under the guise of the D.A.R.E.[16] program. They take two days out of this program to indoctrinate the children against their parents by teaching them that, in their humanistic viewpoint, what their parents are doing is wrong. They tell the children they should report their parents if they get a spanking and *hand out their business cards with a number for the children to call!* In another nearby school district, they are showing a specially made

---

[16]Drug Abuse Resistance Education

video to grade schoolers, once again teaching your child that spanking is child abuse. Who knows exactly what they are doing it in your public school! One thing you can be sure of, they are there.

RELEASING CHILDREN TO THE CUSTODY OF SOCIAL SERVICES

If you must keep your child in public school, understand that you have virtually no protection against the system. As long as they have physical custody of the child, they will relinquish your child to any state agency that simply asks for him. They will do so without requiring the state to produce a warrant, without verifying the child's story, and without notifying you.

If you try to hold the school responsible for turning your child over, you'll find that the immunity laws protect them against any criminal or civil prosecution for doing so, especially if they were the ones who reported the alleged child abuse. You have absolutely no recourse!

NEGATIVE PEER PRESSURE

In truth, there is little positive peer pressure outside of the home or possibly the church. Even if you restrict what your children watch on television, their friends parents' don't, and this negative influence bleeds over onto your child when he's with his friends. The same goes for music, toys, video games, movies, and any other popular culture phenomenon. When your child is rubbing elbows with his school buddies for six or eight hours a day, some of it is bound to rub off on your little darling.

I remember once going to watch my son at a ball game and he didn't know I was there. His behavior was obnoxious, unruly, and just plain bratty! Where on earth did he get the idea it was all right to behave this way, I wondered? He didn't learn it at home, and he knew it was wrong. He wouldn't do that around his family. I realized that what had influenced his behavior came from outside the home. I noticed some of his teammates sassing adults, behaving badly and being as bratty as Eric. The difference was, these children were sassing their parents and acting up while their parents watched without a care. It has become socially acceptable for children to behave so disrespectfully, and Eric admired it enough to emulate it. But only while I wasn't around.

At first, this behavior may be limited to their circle of peers, but eventually, it will make its way into your home. At that point, you will have to confront it. This confrontation could turn into an ugly run-in with Social Services.

If his friends have lenient parents, they will be right there to encourage your child to turn you in, and he just might agree. After all, you probably are too strict, and therefore probably abusive, compared to other parents.

Children do not automatically have the maturity or wisdom to reject bad behaviors, and we, as parents must protect them from having to make these choices until they are mature enough to reject what is wrong.

PROFILING CHILDREN AND FAMILIES

There is a dangerous trend happening in schools now. They are profiling your child and your family. This is done through the means of a so-called academic tests and curriculum that the child is often led to believe he is required to take. Be extremely wary of any exam that requires your approval, I personally wouldn't approve. These tests are often given without your knowledge. After all, the school will only get in trouble if you find out, and they are very careful to make sure you don't find out about them.

These "tests" and classes run the gamut of social

subjects, none of which has anything to do with academics, and usually bear academic sounding names so as not to arouse any suspicion. Many are developed by psychological experts with the intention of gathering personal information about the child and his family. With the information revealed in these tests and classes, authorities know what your family's beliefs and values are, your methods of discipline, your lifestyle, and your child's and even your psychology. The results are not always accurate because sometimes the child misreads the questions, but they are treated as if they were accurate. The results can be used to undermine parental authority and even harass targeted parents and organizations.[17]

As a parent, you are never informed of these tests or their results. They are illegal under federal law but unless you know about them you cannot fight this invasion of your family's privacy. There are many documented instances where the child is instructed not to inform the parents of the contents of certain tests and classes, thereby keeping it a dark and dirty education secret. Ask your children.

One last bombshell: The results are not confidential, and are most likely going to be forwarded to a national database.[18]

POSSIBLE DEFENSES

There is little you can do to defend your family against anything the public and many private schools will do when it comes to reporting reasonable discipline as suspected child abuse except to keep your child out of the

---

[17]Educating for the New World Order, B. K. Eakman, Halcyon House, 1992

[18]Ibid.

school. As I said before, if you leave your child in school, anything you might do to prevent yourself from being investigated is likely to be in vain. There are, however, a few suggestions that might help keep your family intact. Note that I said might. And a lot of the responsibility will be placed on the child. This can be chancy so you have to make the decision if you are willing to take that risk or not, especially in light of the fact that children have little sense of what should be private and what should be reported. The schools and social workers will exploit this naivete to their advantage, and blow an innocuous incident out of proportion.

First, you must explain to the child the difference between abuse and discipline, between beating and spanking. The schools aren't going to do it for you. They are teaching the children that spanking is abuse. Assure the child that if he is abused according to the legal definition, he should report it, but if he's not, he shouldn't try to gain sympathy by exaggerating the spanking or other discipline he got.

You must also make sure he doesn't talk to the counselor at school about anything that goes on in the family. Talks with school counselors should be limited to school issues. If he needs to talk to someone about personal problems, he should tell you and you can promise that you will take him to a pastor or counselor of your choosing. You can then choose a therapist that won't create a conflict with your values or create an adversarial situation between you and your child. School counselors support the government's and education's agenda, not the family.

Children need to be taught that they are not required to talk to any counselor, teacher, police officer or other authority figure if they don't want to. In the event he found himself confronted by questioning adults, I told my son to simply say "I want my parents. I don't want to talk to anyone without my parents here," and nothing else. Fortunately, he never had to employ this tactic. I'm sure it would have been pretty scary to not answer probing questions from adults, especially when he is supposed to respect their authority. It's debatable whether a child would be able to hold out for his parents to get there.

The children should also be told the consequences of making a false report or even an insinuation of abuse. Despite what the teacher or counselor promises, the parent will get in trouble. The child will be removed from the home and visitation with parents and siblings will be very restricted at best and forbidden at the worst. Parental rights can and have been terminated, and the child is never allowed to see his parents again. Even if these worst case scenarios don't occur, the family will be burdened with expensive legal fees, court ordered counseling and parenting classes, and even risk losing their jobs. This puts the family under severe financial and emotional stress. Divorces have been known to occur and the parent-child bond of trust and parental authority is dissolved. How much of this you tell your child is up to you. You know your child best. But if you can avoid laying this kind of burden on your child, why wouldn't you?

Some largely untried options include informing the school in writing that you reserve your parental rights and do not authorize them to relinquish custody of your child to anyone other than yourself, and that they are not permitted to interview or question the child without you or your representative present. Inform them that their failure to comply with your demands will result in a Title 42 (more about this later) lawsuit being filed against every party who violates your rights. Being basically untried, it is questionable whether such tactics would be effective.

You could also get the school board involved by

questioning their procedures for reporting suspected child abuse and requiring them to differentiate between reasonable and legal disciplinary techniques and actual abuse before making a report. This position will probably be frowned upon by the school's lawyers; they devised the reporting policy to protect the school from lawsuits for failing to report abuse, and have exceeded the letter and the spirit of the law in their desire to cover their own backsides. The school board can make sure the reporting policy is not indiscriminate and over-broad, but that it complies with the legal requirements and no more. If they won't, then maybe you should consider running for a school board seat, or, once again institute a Title 42 action personally against the individuals of the school board for violating your rights.

ALTERNATIVES TO PUBLIC SCHOOL

What about private schools? Many are just as suspect. Most are, after all, accredited by the state and accept state money. The teachers may be members of the extremely liberal National Education Association. They have the same attitudes and agenda as public schools.

If your church runs a school, it may be OK; chances are pretty good that your values will not be contradicted. But the more progressive churches have placed liberal interpretations on scriptures dealing with corporal punishment. These churches are likely to cooperate fully with a social worker's demands, no matter how unfounded the allegation.

Even though the more fundamental church schools may exhibit more common sense when encountering a possible allegation of abuse, they can still be intimidated into surrendering custody of your child. This might be forestalled by educating your pastor and principal about your rights and getting their cooperation in standing up for them when confronted by a social worker.

If your church doesn't run a school, and you cannot home-school, talk to them about starting one. Then get involved with it. You have much more control over what happens in a situation if you are there to exert your rights.

The best solution is to home-school. With all the well-designed curriculum available for home-schoolers, it is not as scary or difficult as you have been led to believe. It could well be one of the most rewarding things you have ever done.

When you home-school, you have physical custody of your children. The strategies outlined later in this book are most effective when you have physical control over your children and their surroundings. You determine where your child goes and who he speaks with.

A University of Florida study has shown that home-schooled children socialize better than their public-school peers, without the negative influences of peer pressure. Since contact with other children is limited, you can better protect against the insidious infiltration of conflicting values. As the child gets older his outside contact naturally increases, but this occurs at a time when he is better able to resist negative influences.

These negative influences seem to show up in middle school. How many parents have seen their adorable child turn into a monster, virtually overnight? He's twelve, and he's developed a bad attitude and a smart mouth. He won't do his school work, and he gets in trouble with other boys his age at school. This rarely happens with home-schooled children. Home-schooled children are calmer, less excitable. You can drastically reduce the negative impact of peer pressure, and of offensive subject matter, when you home-school your child. This reduces the need for strict discipline that could open the door to child abuse charges, and limits his contact with extremist child savers who would indoctrinate him against your values and "protect" him from his caring and concerned parents.

NO COMPROMISE

There is a word defined by Webster as: "someone obstinately and intolerantly devoted to his own beliefs." The word is bigot. Sometimes it is good to be bigoted. Your adherence to your core values is one of those times.

Whatever you have determined to be the rules in your home, the expectations of conduct from family members should be inflexible. They can vary according to each person, his abilities, his maturity, his needs, and his responsibilities, but your rules should be firm. If the rules are broken, the consequences must be certain.

This is difficult to accomplish, especially with so many against you. It might seem easier just to back down and conform. That's just what the child savers want. That is why they target people like you. But the only way you can instill these values into your children is to live them yourself, without backing down, without compromising.

If you compromise, they win, and your children lose. If you back down, you will lose the respect of your children. Give them the limits they need, and enforce them fairly. Be strong.

Do not buckle under the yolk of politically correct discipline. You know best what works for your children. You must stick by your plan of discipline as if it were the Ten Commandments written in stone. God gave those children to you, not to the state, and not to some social working busybody who thinks she's smarter than you. They are your responsibility and you must answer for how you handled that responsibility, the state won't, and neither will that self-righteous busybody. Since God entrusted those precious blessings to you, who would question His wisdom in granting you this special gift but an absolute fool?

DIVIDE AND CONQUER

Both parents must present a united front before the children. You must not present any crack that the child could wedge open. If you disagree about a discipline situation, do not argue about it in front of the children. This must be resolved privately, and then enforced jointly.

Do not permit your children to pit one parent against the other. They can only do this if both parents are not firmly united in authority over the children. One parent must not override the punishment of another. If the punishment has been changed, the parent that issued it must be the one to change it. This eliminates the perception of one parent undermining the authority of the other.

Finally, both parents must present a united front to any attempts at investigation by the department of Social Services and law enforcement. These agencies will also try to get both parents to contradict each other or rat each other out, usually by threatening you with prosecution or loss of the children if you don't turn the other one in. Another common ploy is that the social worker will allow the child to return home if dad moves out and dad never visits. If dad was abusive, that's understandable, but when the charges are false, it is devastating to the marriage and the needs of the child. If you are aware of these tactics, it is easier to stand together against these attacks. In truth, they will probably batter at you even harder, but you can learn how to rebuff their attacks and preserve your family.

BE THERE

I once heard a sixteen-year-old girl on a talk radio show give an astonishingly wise observation. She was asked what parents should do to keep their teenagers out of trouble. Her response was simple: "Be there."

Most parents can understand this with their babies. Babies need constant attention. But babies need more than that. You can influence their intelligence, their behavior and their attitudes from birth in a way that no babysitter or child care center can. As *you* care for your baby, you are nurturing a bond that could become critical when they reach adolescence. Your interaction and your touch all contribute to their intelligence and the rapport that you build with that child. No day care provider, babysitter or nanny will care for that child as lovingly as you do. Your child needs your touch.

As they become toddlers, they see you reacting rationally to problems, rather than other toddlers having temper tantrums. They learn from you how to behave. They learn your wishes, your temperament, and your expectations. And they see you in all your phases, at your best and at your worst, instead of just your worst after a hard day at work when you are hardest to like. They learn to like you.

As they grow into grade school age, you are there to instill the proper values, instead of one of their peers. You can nip a potential problem in the bud rather than discovering and trying to resolve it after it has become serious. And who better to praise their accomplishments than mom and dad. You can instill a sense of pride for doing the right thing and for accomplishing difficult tasks, reinforcing their own self-worth.

By the time your children are teenagers, you might think that they don't need as much supervision. Remember the sixteen-year-old on the talk radio show?

You need to be there for teenagers because teenagers are more needful in many ways than babies. If you don't believe me, just ask a policeman on patrol.

According to police, most teenage crime and behavior problems are seen as a lack of parenting rather than a lack of discipline. In other words, if the parents aren't there, they can't be parenting. Most parents have no idea what their absence means to a teenager.

I've had one police officer observe that when both parents work, they leave the responsibility of the house to their teenage son or daughter, saying it's his or her responsibility. These children must be responsible for the younger siblings, do the laundry, make dinner, and whatever else needs to be done. Who can blame them when these teenagers get it into their head that they are entitled to the privileges of adulthood, too?

So, in the absence of their parents, and without leaving the comforts of home in many cases, they experiment with drugs, sex and alcohol. Without their parent's supervision, they turn to crime for a cheap thrill or for cash to support a growing drug habit. These are kids whose parents are the pillars of the community. Tax paying, churchgoing, all-around nice people. But nobody's watching the teenager, and nobody's there to talk to him, or guide him. And we adults wonder why they make foolish decisions.

And the parents, appalled at what their son is doing, react with harsh but lawful discipline, and once again, Social Services can be called to intervene.

The situation where parents are pitted against a willful teenager can once again be largely prevented simply by being there. As a parent in attendance, you can address problems while they are still small, and without getting confrontational about it. This is the opportunity to finish building his character and to encourage him to develop his own sense of responsibility, all under your supervision and guidance. Most important, you can continue building the bridges of communication, preventing the need for him to take his problems outside of the home and risk opening up your family to investigation. If you are home with him, you control his environment, therefore, you prevent serious problems.

Today, most families cannot survive on a single income, so both parents work. This is why so many children are left home alone for several hours each day. You already know that unsupervised children spell trouble, and for older children, day care is not an option.

One alternative is working different shifts. If husband and wife can work different shifts, that would leave one parent home with the children at all times. The downside is that it doesn't leave much time for the parents to spend together, but it has proven to be an effective solution for many families while the children are home.

Another option is for one or both of the parents to telecommute during certain days or hours of the day, so they can be home with the children. Some companies also offer flex-time, allowing the employee to go in early or start later to accommodate the family's needs.

If you are among the growing ranks of self-employed individuals, you've got a head start. As your own boss, you determine company policies. My husband owns an upholstery shop, and we actually home-schooled our children at the shop. How many bosses will let you bring your children to work with you every day? If you work out of your home, you can adjust your hours to accommodate your child's lessons.

You can also recruit members of your extended family to supervise your children. Grandma or Aunt Sandy, if she has the same values as you, is almost as good as mom or dad being home by keeping the supervision all in the family.

THE MYTH OF TEENAGE REBELLION

Teenage rebellion is a relatively recent manifestation perpetrated by contemporary "experts." Close examination reveals that the more lax authority becomes, the more profound teenage rebellion becomes.

This particular myth actually encourages teenagers to rebel, by giving them "social permission" to do so. In fact, it has become expected. Given this kind of expectation, who can blame teenagers for indulging in it? Even if a particular youth is not inclined to be overtly rebellious, his peers will pressure him to rebel against authority.

This rebellion gives them social permission to be irresponsible, and even to fail at anything they attempt, supposedly without recrimination. When the parents don't buy into this fallacy and attempt to enforce their expectations, thereby going against the social grain, a confrontation brews.

Because the child has social permission to fail, he also has social permission to disobey his parents, especially if his parents attempt to enforce their expectations with traditional disciplinary tactics.

Ultimately, teenage rebellion can be used to break up the family, remove the child from the home, and prosecute the parents. Can you see why it is advantageous for the experts to continue to support this myth?

DAMAGE CONTROL FOR ORDINARY ACCIDENTS

Children have accidents. Children get ill. These normal occurances can be misinterpreted and become potential reports of abuse. My sister-in-law's young daughter had a bed wetting problem which caused a vaginal yeast infection in the child. Her mother had to apply medication to the affected area. The child's innocent remark, made while she watched a day care worker change her brother's diaper, about her mommy touching her bottom, resulted in a horrifying rash of allegations and an intrusive and offensive investigation. All this happened in spite of a sworn statement by the child's doctor, verifying her condition and the prescribed treatment. The mother lost her job because of this incident.

As a parent, you need to know how to protect yourself from this too-common knee-jerk reactionary attack. The real tragedy is that this subject must even be broached.

In the event that your child suffers an accidental injury that requires medical attention, do not take the child to the emergency room unless his injury is life-threatening. Emergency room personnel are required by law to report suspected child abuse cases. When they are treating unfamiliar patients, they are more likely to assume an injury has been caused as a result of child abuse and report it. With relatively minor injuries, like simple fractures, sprains, minor head injuries, and cuts requiring stitches, you are better off taking your child to your family doctor for treatment. He is familiar with you as the parent, and with the child's medical history, and can assess the injury in the correct context. He is less likely to view a childhood accident as child abuse, thereby protecting you and your family. This personal knowledge can save you a lot of heartache and expense.

If your family doctor decides you need to take the child to the hospital, you will be much better protected than if you brought the child to the hospital first. He will notify the emergency room to prepare for the child's arrival, and give them his assessment of the injury. Since your child had already been seen by another professional, it is unlikely that the injury will be reported as abuse.

As an example of how an emergency room visit can be dangerous: There is a single mother in Colorado whose young daughter accidentally ingested Tylenol. The mother rushed her to the emergency room, where they waited for more than four hours for the girl to be treated. This delay in treatment resulted in the child requiring an overnight hospital stay. The mother was reported for child neglect, even though she sought lifesaving treatment for her child, and is currently in the process of having all parental rights terminated. Because the child was in the physical custody of the hospital, they turned her over to the department of Social Services without hesitation, and the mother wasn't allowed to see her.

Even in light of this horror story, it is better to take the child to the emergency room than to risk losing him to an accident. The issue of physical custody can be resolved when the child is ready to leave the hospital, and you can be prepared to assert your parental rights under those circumstances. It would not be wise to leave the child's side while he is in the hospital. Some overzealous social worker might just whisk him away in your absence.

Some children have a chronic disorder or a disease that causes injuries which could be construed as having resulted from child abuse. Epilepsy is one such disease. If your child is affected by a medical disorder that causes injury, notify anyone who has regular contact with your child and who might be compelled to report child abuse, of your child's medical condition in writing, and of the possible effects of his affliction, such as cuts, bruises, etc. Then, advise them after he has experienced an episode and how violent it was. A doctor's affidavit for this type of affliction would be invaluable. You can also keep him at home for a day or two, until the effects of his episode have faded.

If your child is receiving medical treatments that could cause sores, bruises, or other injuries, it might be wise to obtain a statement from the treating physician to verify the effects of the treatment. This can also be used to prevent charges of child abuse, or can be used as evidence to defend yourself in the event you are investigated.

CHAPTER 3

THE MEDIA

"Time has convinced me on one thing: Television is for appearing on-not for looking at." Noel Coward

Look at your children while they watch television or listen to rock music. Their eyes are glazed, jaws slack, they are intensely focused. They don't hear you when you address them. Why?

They are being psychologically manipulated with very subtle yet sophisticated brainwashing techniques. Their tender minds are especially vulnerable to this manipulation, where the adult mind is not so easily influenced. However, adults are not immune to this seductive influence either. Being aware of its existence contributes greatly to being able to resist the suggestion.

Once aware of the manipulation, you can discount the effects, but children are naive, and unable to discern what is happening to them. It is up to you to protect them from these manipulative influences.

ROCK MUSIC

Titillating. Exciting. Hypnotic. Suggestive. Violent. You can barely understand the words of some songs over the thundering beat and screaming guitars. But the negative, violent and immoral lyrics, coupled with the deafening, hypnotic beat make their way into the subconscious mind, affecting your child's attitudes and values.

Recognizing the negative influence, we never allowed heavy metal or acid-type rock music in our home. But Eric went out and bought himself some of this forbidden music, recommended by a friend, and listened to it secretly. We were able to pinpoint exactly when he started listening to it because his behavior changed dramatically. He exhibited extreme mood swings and sank into depressed episodes where we couldn't motivate him. He lost interest in things that he used to enjoy. He exhibited more anger and resisted our rules and authority. He became secretive and quit communicating with us.

I found the tapes. Not wishing to condemn them unfairly, I listened to them, using my eighteen years as a musician to analyze the music carefully. This music was discordant, dominated by the bone-jarring beat. The words were difficult to understand, the melody virtually impossible to follow. I read the lyrics on the cover of the tape. They were foul, full of disjointed, negative thoughts, perversions, and violence. The ugliest examples of human nature were glorified and pounded into my young son's impressionable mind with a driving, hypnotic beat.

Needless to say, the tapes were confiscated, and he earned unannounced spot checks of his tape player and tapes. His mood and attitude improved, but he still yearned for the forbidden music. He said it relaxed him. I believe it did, just as it was designed to. All the better to influence him, my dear.

TELEVISION

My beloved mother-in-law was born and raised in France. Many of her family still reside there, and she communicates with them often.

American television is very popular in Europe. Being a naturalized American, my mother-in-law has the proper perspective regarding the Hollywood portrayal of American life on television. The average Frenchman doesn't.

Consequently, many of them actually believe that our soap operas are an accurate representation of the average American's life. These are educated adults, they're not stupid, but they have no way of knowing that soap operas bear only the remotest resemblance to real life in America.

If intelligent adults can make this mistake, can't our impressionable young children be influenced by the values and actions depicted on television, also? An August 18, 1996 *Parade Magazine* poll shows that the issues that are presented positively on television, such as single parents being able to raise a family, availability of condoms in schools, government spending on AIDS research and nationalized health care, and the promotion of premarital sex and abortion are supported by a majority of teenagers. Would they support such immoral issues if they were portrayed negatively in the media? Well, they used to be. I don't think the entertainment media is a reflection of our society. I think our society is influenced by the values presented in the media.

What are our children watching on television these days? What are they absorbing from the shows they watch?

SITCOMS

Today's sitcoms abound with smart-mouthed children who are encouraged to behave disrespectfully to their parents, assuming they even have parents. We are often treated to scenes of the "offended" youngster running from the room while the parent vainly commands them to return. Having issued the command, the parent then fails to enforce the command. Consequences? Usually an apology from the parent to the child. There is no mention of the child's disobedience, no enforcement of the rules, no discipline at all.

Children are portrayed as being able to outsmart their parents. They trap their parents in lies or other wrongdoing, thereby winning themselves a reprieve from their own deserved punishment.

Other shows are dripping with sexual innuendos and sight gags. Some glorify premarital relationships and loose morals. The rapidly increasing homosexual situations are portrayed as positive. Lying, cheating, stealing, and other wrongs are justifiable depending on the circumstances. In other words, relative morality reigns instead of absolute right and wrong.

If your children see this, is it possible they think everyone else have such wimpy parents and they wish they did, too? You must be too strict, and probably abusive. This type of comparison can set the uncompromising righteous parent up for child abuse allegations.

CHILDREN'S SHOWS

Have you ever sat down and watched the cartoons and children's shows your kids watch? They aren't the same things we watched while we were growing up.

Today's children are being systematically indoctrinated into the occult, New Ageism, and rabid environmentalism. Our planet, and its wild creatures, is more important than people. Competition is portrayed as bad, as is anyone who promotes individuality. Many themes are Socialist/Marxist with an environmental overtone. The supernatural abounds, with spirits and tokens of witchcraft. Values are twisted, with moral relativism being the measure of right and wrong. Even Sesame Street is getting very politically correct and tolerant, espousing socialist values, diversity, and globalism.

This is yet another, pervasive influence that you must fight, because it conflicts with Biblical values. Because of this, my children were not allowed to watch most children's programming, including contemporary cartoons. We only allowed them to watch the older Warner Brothers and other similar cartoons.

PRIME TIME

It's amusing to see how the networks will place a warning about violence before a Star Trek episode, but blatant sex on more offensive shows is rarely warned of.

We see characters casually hopping into bed with each other without the benefit of marriage. Is it any wonder young people today forgo marriage and simply live together?

The conflict of values presented during prime time is often resolved without using any measure of right and wrong. The end often justifies the means.

People are thoughtlessly killed, just for the thrill.

Victimhood is glorified. Mediocrity is extolled. Even the commercials insist on immediate gratification and materialism; buy more, buy bigger, be attractive because of what you own, charge it. Obviously, these are not great values for building a society with character and integrity.

One fourteen year old girl made a false accusation of sexual abuse against her stepfather. She shortly recanted, saying she got the idea from her sex-ed class in school and from watching Montel Williams. Television does influence our dear children in the most negative way. The agents of the state did not believe her recanted story, and she remains in foster care.

PUTTING CHILDREN FIRST

An innocuous phrase. Altruistic. Surely a holy endeavor. Who would condemn such a righteous cause? Who would even question such a benign phrase?

I would. This is an insidious campaign

coincidentally conducted in concert with the UN Convention on the Rights of the Child (and all it's associated spinoffs) that is designed to usurp parental rights and authority. It is propaganda, woven from the lies of statistics which only record 'reported cases of child abuse' and disregards the fact that 60 to 90% of those 'reported' cases are unfounded. It is a masterful marketing scheme, blasted across television screen around the country, designed to 'reeducate' people into thinking children are more important than anything (except for the convenience of the mother if she chooses to abort an unborn child, oops, I mean fetus). It makes children think the world revolves around them (not a good notion for children to have). Its entire focus is off-center, highlighting the children and excluding the parents thereby invalidating the family as a viable union.

There is no wisdom or logic to this reasoning. How can children always be the number one most important thing? On the television show "*COPS*" you often hear a cop asking a mother: who is more important, your husband or your children? Mother knows she must say the children, or the cop will take her babies away. But in truth, the husband could take priority, for he supports the family and he will be with her long after the children have grown and moved away. Without dad, the kids will suffer. Why must parents make that choice?

I am not disputing the importance that children must take in the family. The raising of children should be a priority for parents, probably more so than it is in most families. The key issue here is the family. This devious campaign is encouraging outsiders to assume a role they are not ordained to take, by intruding into the realm of the family and usurping the parents' prerogatives.

I have seen commercials advocating 'children first', urging children and teens to develop relationships and dialogs with teachers, coaches, mentors, and various other concerned and 'enlightened' adults. Oddly, they are not encouraged to develop a relationship with their own parents, or to even learn to communicate with their parents. The same message is repeated to our children in our public schools. What's wrong with this picture?

This is a classic example of how this campaign is seeking to replace the parent's role with the 'it takes a village to raise a child' pattern of raising children. God didn't command villages to 'be fruitful and multiply', or provide governments with scriptural advice on how to raise children. God charged parents with that responsibility. Based on my observations, the 'village' is full of idiots, and I don't think the 'village idiots' can raise children as effectively or lovingly as the vast majority of parents can.

Take for example the recent announcement regarding rating television shows. Parents have overwhelmingly demanded to know the content of the shows, i.e., whether there is profanity, nudity, casual sex scenes, homosexual situations, graphic violence, etc. The village idiots in Hollywood and Washington, D.C. just recently insisted parents should accept the movie-style age-based rating system that has failed miserably with parents around the country. I know I couldn't let my children watch PG-13 movies without pre-screening. I never knew when some naked piece of private anatomy would be flaunted or foul language uttered. And this is ok for 13 year olds? Not in my book. But it is ok in the Village Idiot's book.

You may say I'm too old-fashioned. As a parent, it's my prerogative. This country isn't suffering a societal crisis because too many children were raised with strict morals and conservative values.

The 'Children First' campaign is just Big Brother

telling us that parents can't do a good enough job raising their own children. The ever-benevolent and wise Big Brother decrees that the village idiots have the right and the obligation to interfere with the way you raise your children. The 'Children First' campaign is trying to subtly condition us to accept the doctrine that our children, borne of our own bodies, belong to the state.

Unbelievably extreme? Not any more. In spite of Supreme Court rulings to the contrary, some state courts have recently ruled that the state has a 'moral imperative' to insure that our children are raised according to the best interests of the state, regardless if the state's interests conflict with the parents' values. 'Putting Children First' means ignoring one of the most important needs of children by putting parents last.

There's an adage in the computer industry: Garbage in, Garbage out. A computer only does what you tell it to do. Period. Whatever you put into it, that's what it returns to you. Your children are exactly the same. You must be careful what you put into these young skulls full of mush if you hope to have them mature into righteous adults, and have them respect your authority while they're maturing. The best defense is a good offense; restrict and monitor what they watch on TV. If you can keep the garbage out of their heads, you won't have to fight against it later.

CHAPTER 4

APPLYING DISCIPLINE IN LOVE

"We never know the love of the parent till we become parents ourselves." Henry Ward Beecher

PROTECT YOURSELF

In today's society, you must discipline defensively. You never know when you'll be blind sided by allegations of child abuse. If you have disciplined defensively, you won't be caught off guard.

The most important defense is to stick to your clearly defined plan of discipline. The interventionist child savers love to portray parents as getting out of control and madly beating their children. Your emotionally charged response to this obvious and provocative lie simply supports their allegations. However, your calm response, coupled with your rational demonstration of your well-thought out discipline plan can make them appear rabid and unreasonable in their unnecessary protection of your children.

This plan will, by necessity, be somewhat flexible. Common sense dictates that what works for a two-year-old will not work for an eleven-year-old, what works for your complacent child will not work for your strong willed child.

You will have to take into account the age and temperament of each child. Make sure your discipline is appropriate to the age and the offense of the child. However, as I mentioned earlier, it is best to save spanking for willful disobedience.

How do you determine willful disobedience?

When your two year old looks at you with an evil glint in his eye or a stubborn set to his jaw as he reaches for the forbidden knickknack, this is willful disobedience. He knows it is forbidden, but he's going to touch it anyway. Punishment, swift and sure, is required.

But, if he spills his milk at supper, he's just had an accident. His hands are still learning the mechanics of drinking from a cup. This is not usually a punishable offense.

However, if your eight-year-old spills his milk at supper, after you've told him to quit fooling around at the table, he has disobeyed. Would spanking be appropriate?

That depends on many variables: How often has this happened, how much of it was attributable to carelessness and how much to willful disobedience? How effective are spankings with this child? Would another method be more effective? You can probably think of more.

Factors that absolutely should not be considered are: Did you have a bad day at work or on the road, are you dead tired, was this the last straw, did you just get fired or sued or whatever? Your mood should not be a factor in determining the severity of the punishment you inflict on your child. He is not responsible for your bad day, so don't take it out on him. This is the hardest time to be fair, so you must be strongest when you are at your weakest.

I've found that making the child responsible for correcting his damage is highly effective in preventing future damage. When Jacob was two, he colored the wall with his crayons. I made him wash the wax off. He cried for more than two hours, doing a lousy job, but I made sure he scrubbed as best as his little toddler hands could manage. He never colored on anything but paper again.

When Eric was five, he chewed up the arm on my

wooden rocking chair. I told him I was angry that he damaged my birthday present, bought him a sanding block and sandpaper, and made him sand all the gouges out of the wood. It took hours, fraught with tears, but he never chewed or pounded or scratched on another piece of furniture again. A broken window - the window breaker buys the new glass and replaces it. Hole in the wall - he calls the drywall man and pays for it, all on his own. Where do they get the money? They use their birthday money or they have to earn it, just like anyone else. I give them options for earning it but the choice is up to them. These are consequences of negative behavior.

Was I angry? Darn right. Sometimes I felt like really belting them. But my goal was to teach them not to do anything that was stupid or wrong, and washing crayon off a wall is a whole lot more distasteful, and effective, than a few swats on the bottom. Sometimes spanking is just a manifestation of lazy parenting.

Alternative disciplines can still be construed as abusive. Jacob, again the willful two year old, refused to eat his beef stew one night. He'd eaten it before, but he was asserting his independence this night. Was mommy going to get into a power struggle with a strong willed toddler? No way! Spanking him wouldn't make him eat his supper. Spanking doesn't make a child do anything, it is a punishing tool rather than a teaching tool. Instead, I set the rules: He could get down without eating it, but . . . he couldn't have anything but water until breakfast, and he would get the stew for breakfast. He decided to get down. Now comes the hard part for mommy and daddy.

Shortly after dinner, Jacob was hungry, he wanted a cookie. Would that break the rules? You bet, no cookies allowed. Oh! The pooched out pout and the pitiful tears. I reminded him of his decision and then told him if he was going to be crabby, he could go to bed early. Since I'd proved to him previously that I meant what I said, he quit being crabby.

The next morning, Jacob bounced awake with his usual morning smile and ran to his high chair, eager for breakfast. I put the warmed over beef stew in front of him. Shocked surprise was rapidly replaced with a glower. He didn't want the stew. I reminded him of the rules, and *he decided* to wait until lunch.

Lunch was a repeat of breakfast. By supper time, he'd only had water to drink for the past 24 hours. That's a long time for a two-year-old. Was this child abuse? Not in my opinion. Rather, it was a non-confrontational and very effective method to teach him to eat what he was served or go hungry.

Many child-savers would disagree. This episode would have been portrayed as my deliberately and maliciously withholding food from him for more than 24 hours. This exaggerated depiction bears only the smallest kernel of resemblance to what actually happened. I could have been in danger of having my child taken away, even without any evidence of abuse or neglect.

The story ends happily. Jacob loved pizza, so I made pizza for supper, but I served him the beef stew. He looked at the pizza that mommy and daddy were eating and gobbled down his stew. Then he had some pizza. Manipulative? Sure it was, but it was pretty hard on this mom to see her little boy being so stubborn, so I made sure *he wanted* to eat that stew by making something else that he couldn't resist. He never refused to eat what was served again. This strategy had the added bonus that he rarely tried to out-stubborn me on anything else either.

Was this luck? Absolutely not. I knew Jacob was strong willed. I knew I had to get this will under control while he was small, otherwise I couldn't hope to do it when he was older. This is why it is so important that you know your child's temperament. I also knew that spanking would be counterproductive in this circumstance, so it took some creative parenting to arrive at an effective solution.

Other techniques I've found effective over the years include, running to the end of our property and back (or laps around the block), digging up cactus (or weeds) by the wheelbarrow full on our 40-acre property, watering our 125 seedling trees on our 40 acres - one milk jug full per tree, and digging a root cellar by hand (this took the two boys two years to dig a ten foot square, six foot deep hole). Each of these "punishments" has the virtue of building a strong body and a good work ethic. Unbelievably, I've been told by a social worker that making my children run was abuse! How inconsistent - what about gym teachers then?

A note about today's most popular technique - the time out. After researching numerous "experts'" glowing reports on giving children a time out, I have found one glaring deficiency. It doesn't work! In seminars, when parents complain that they've tried it, they're told they did it wrong, or they must be patient, or something similar. The process of time out is never to blame. And when it has failed, the parent is never offered an effective alternative, but is instructed to stick with the time out.

Suppose the parents did do it wrong. If the technique is so difficult to do right that most parents can't get the hang of it, what's its value? It's useless. The real problem is that these experts can't admit that this technique is a complete flop. Kids love timeouts. No pain, no embarrassment, no consequences. Therefore, no effect. No wonder we are forced to endure a generation of undisciplined brats. If you are looking for effective alternative discipline methods, you'll have to be more creative than these "time out" advocates.

Having spent all this time finding ways to avoid spanking doesn't mean you must eliminate spanking. Maybe your child is like Jacob, who needed more spankings than Eric. All we had to do was make Eric stand in the corner and he'd boo-hoo muddy tears all over the wall. He was heartbroken to stand in the corner. Jacob didn't care. He'd play imaginary games. But he was profoundly and positively affected by some firmly placed swats on the backside.

You decide what offenses are spanking offenses. In my house, lying was always a spanking offense. Other spankings were usually administered after our previous, "more creative" punishments for a particular type of offense had failed. We also felt that a first offense was almost never a spanking offense, giving the child a chance to learn a new rule.

What does a spanking mean? Obviously you cannot administer the same spanking you'd give your ten-year-old to your two-year-old; it could be abusive. I personally believe you can administer a stinging slap to the face of a smart-mouthed, adult sized teenager, but you'd probably injure your four-year-old doing the same thing. Your punishment must be adjusted to account for the physical size and development of your child.

One thing you don't do is grab the child's arm and swat him as he's dangling. You might injure his shoulder, and it's too hard to control where you might strike him as he's dancing around at the end of your grip.

Do you use your hand or an implement of some sort? It's really a no-win decision. Experts say using your hand makes the child fearful of your hand. I disagree, especially if you follow the rules of explaining the infraction and what they can expect for it. Implements like paddles or belts absolutely will become instruments of torture in the courtroom as far as a prosecutor is concerned. You have to decide.

I used my hand on small, unprotected bottoms, it gave me more control over the strength of the blow and did not injure me. As children get older, their bottoms become remarkably tough, and my hand didn't make a significant impression on their attitude. Commonly used implements include wooden spoons (easily broken on bottoms), ping pong paddles, specially made spanking paddles, belts, and the wicked looking martinet. We used the martinet. It was soft suede, designed to sting but not injure. The prosecution had a field day with it in my husband's child abuse case, but it failed to move the jury to convict him. I bring it to my seminars and proudly display it as a trophy of our victory.

Your safest choice would be to use what the state law authorizes schools to use, if your schools are allowed to spank. It would be easiest to justify your use of a spanking implement that the state has authorized in its statutes.

You must also be sure that your children clearly understand your rules and the consequences for disobedience. This gives them the opportunity to obey or disobey. If they understand that you are bound by the same rules they are, you cannot be blamed for their bad decisions. If the rules say punishment for disobedience, and they disobey, then you are bound by the rules to punish that disobedience. These rules are not made to be broken or negotiated away. You must be consistent. If your children can depend on you to punish disobedience, then they will be less inclined to disobey. You will eventually need to punish less often.

Finally, if your child misbehaves in public and requires a spanking, don't administer it in public. You can be sure some well-intentioned busybody will call the police and they will snatch your child right out of the store, or as soon as you return home, and hide him away in foster care. I firmly believe that disobedience must be addressed immediately, but today's social mood makes it too dangerous for you to do it in public. I also believe that if a child embarrasses you in public, you are well within your rights to reciprocate. Embarrass him right back.

Drop what you're doing, leave the cart full of groceries or the toy store or the restaurant or whatever. Calmly drag your (kicking and screaming?) brat out to the car, drive home, and spank his bottom. Then take him back to the store with you, pick up your cart or whatever, look him straight in the eye and say loudly, "I expect you to behave yourself. I do not want to have to drag you out of this store in front of all of these people again. If I must, I'm sure you will not want to come back." I doubt he will ever try dramatic theatrics and tantrums in public again. If he does, he may be testing. Be firm. Be consistent.

Alternatively, you might be able to locate a restroom nearby. If you are able to lock the door so nobody else can enter, do so. Otherwise, administer the spanking when the restroom is deserted. As a last resort, lock yourself in the larger handicap stall for some privacy. There is still a risk because you are still in public, but this option will diminish that risk. If you notice someone following you to read your license plates or trying to identify you in any other way, confront him or her (these busybodies are usually women). Inform them that you have not been abusive according to the state law (it helps if you can cite the statute). Then inform them of the federal penalties and of their civil liability for making a false report. Tell them you'll sue them. Tell them to butt out if you feel like it. Follow them to their car and get their license plate number. If you carry a camera (I do, a disposable camera is small and light), take their picture. Tell them it's so you can identify them for your lawsuit against them. Intimidation works wonders. Then don't go near your own car until they have left the area.

If your child is having tantrums past the age of three, he may require spankings. What you have done previously hasn't worked, and you'd better get it under control now! It will only get worse.

Above all, don't ever make a threat or a promise that you don't keep. This encourages disobedience. If you said, "Johnny, get down or I'll spank you," and Johnny doesn't get down, then you must spank him as you promised. Very shortly Johnny will learn to get down when you tell him.

HOW TO SPANK

When you spank, first explain to the child exactly how he disobeyed. Make sure you get his acknowledgment that he knew the rules and knew he was disobeying.

Then explain the consequences. Tell him exactly how many swats he'll get, and what they'll be administered with.

Have the child explain his understanding of the offense and the consequences. Don't allow excuses.

Have him assume the position you require for his safety. Make sure he understands he is not to move, that you don't want to injure him. We told our children that if they moved or attempted to dodge the spanking, it would earn them extra swats. Administer the spanking without emotion or excessive force, or excessive leniency.

Having finished, it's time for closure. Make sure he understands that the punishment is complete and the offense forgiven. It's time to start with a clean slate. Reassure him of your love. If the child is young, compliment him on his strength in not moving around during the spanking. Give him whatever emotional or physical support he needs. Sometimes, they just need to be held for a while, sometimes they need to be alone. Just let them know you'll be there whenever they need you.

If you need to (I sometimes did), retreat to privacy to heal your own anguish. I've found it really does hurt me more than it hurt them to spank my children. When my husband, Dennis, had to spank one of the boys the first time, he came to me visibly shaken. He confessed he had no idea it was so painful to spank a child he loved. While my son had quickly recovered from the effects of the spanking, Dennis needed comforting and reassurance. Maybe that's why so many parents won't spank, they're too weak or cowardly to do what is right, and are willing to let their children suffer for their weakness.

Put your discipline plan in writing. Include all pertinent information like the maximum number of swats you'll give, what you'll administer them with, for what offenses, etc. You can establish different rules for different sized children. Then, take it to your pastor and have him evaluate it. You'll want to know if it is scriptural and not abusive. Having a respected professional put his seal of approval on your plan of discipline will give you more ammunition to defend yourself against false allegations of abuse.

WARNING SIGNS

OK, you've got it all down. You have a clearly defined plan of discipline. You've carefully considered the age of the child and the infraction. You're fair and consistent, you can't be coaxed or bribed out of doing what is right.

One day, out of the blue, sonny boy says, in a joking matter, "That's child abuse." Ha ha, you laugh along and let it pass.

Big mistake. What we have here is a child who has

learned from somewhere that you are not supposed to spank him, or slap him, or even punish him, and he's testing the waters. Can he make you, by his innuendo, stop what you are doing? He thinks he can. He has just told you that he knows there are people out there who will swoop in to his rescue if he tells them you spank, or if he tells a teeny little lie and makes them think you abuse him. Who's in control here?

What you do now will determine who has control in your family for all time. You must take this "joke" seriously.

If you were about to administer a spanking, you should have a discreet witness to the act, and if possible, have your witness video tape or audio tape the event and all subsequent disciplinary sessions. If sonny boy turns you in for abuse, you'll need these tapes to prove you were not abusive. You could also keep a journal of the offense, the punishment, the witness, and the date. Have your witness note his observations in this journal, too.

Most important, do not let your child know you are recording the event, and do not let him see or hear any of the tapes or journals. He will surely tell the police who would confiscate them for evidence if they charge you with abuse. Sometimes, evidence disappears or is damaged, especially evidence that is damaging to the prosecution.

When I say "if sonny boy turns you in for abuse," I don't necessarily mean he would accuse you directly. He might make an offhand comment to one of his friends, "My dad hit me," and his faithful friend would report it to the school counselor. You're nailed.

He might talk to a teacher at school, who imagines abuse and he does not dissuade her. You're nailed.

He might even deny it all to the police or social services when they respond to the teacher's call. You're still nailed. And sonny boy never made a single accusation of abuse.

These tapes must be secretly made, and kept secret. Hopefully you'll never have to use them.

Oh, you cry, what treachery that I must stoop to spying on my own son. The reality is that your son (or daughter) is being deceived and manipulated by the agents of the state. He doesn't know it. He believes what they tell him. He's too young to know any better. You must protect yourself. In protecting yourself you're protecting your family and your dear sonny boy.

Dads, watch out for daughter dear. These young girls are well trained in all aspects of sexual abuse. Unfortunately, you might have to consider limiting your contact with daughter dear to chaperoned interaction. If your daughter has suddenly "gone wild" or you cannot understand why she is being so defiant or angry, you are seeing a warning sign. Make sure your interaction with her is always in the presence of another adult, preferably your wife. Do not give her the opportunity to accuse you falsely. Mom, keep an eye out and protect your husband from a false accusation. If daughter dear is exhibiting the signs, let her read the letter from Crystal at the end of this book so she can see that once the accusation is made, it cannot be taken back.

When sonny boy makes his joke, or daughter dear makes unsubstantiated hints about daddy touching her, you must confront him or her with the seriousness of the issue. He may become embarrassed. If he does, good. He's still got a conscience. Be straightforward. You must debunk the lies that he's been told by the agents of the state.

First, explain exactly what child abuse is, and how it differs from properly administered discipline or normal touching. Explain to him the state law that allows parents to spank or use whatever force is necessary. These laws can be found in your public library, in the reference section. The reference librarian can help you find them. Make copies of them for your own reference. Use them to prove that the agents of the state are lying to him.

Then explain what abuse is. Abuse serves no purpose in discipline. It is an immature display of temper using violent actions against the child resulting in injury.

Assure him that if he is abused, you would expect him to report it. But he must be sure it is abuse, and not just a selfish retaliation for your just punishment of his disobedience.

Explain to him the consequences of such an allegation. Make sure he understands that once the allegation is made, it cannot be taken back, even if he lied, or just stretched the truth. Nobody will believe he lied. They want to believe that you are an abusive parent.

The social worker will tell him his parents won't get in trouble. It's a lie. They often take the child out of the home and the parents can be taken away to jail in handcuffs. If that happens, they could lose their jobs, their home, and everything they own. The only way they can get children to rat out their parents is to lie to the children. Make sure he understands how dishonest the agents of the state are.

The agents of the state can make it sound fun for the child to be placed in a foster home. It even might be at first. I was in a foster home as a teenager. It's not the same as being with your family. Foster children get abused, too. They are often there just to provide cleaning and babysitting services. I've heard of one case where a homosexual male was a foster parent, and he requested teenage boys. He'd walk around the house naked, and one fifteen year old foster boy was terrified. He pleaded with the judge to be removed from the foster home, but the judge ruled it would be discrimination against the homosexual foster parent. What about the boy's rights? Children's rights and protection are not the issue in child abuse cases. It's about money. Lots of federal money.

They will promise that sonny boy or daughter dear will not be held against their will. They're lying. Your child will not be allowed to come home when he's tired of his game. Your child will be allowed limited and probably supervised visitations with the family if he's lucky. Usually, there is little or no contact allowed. You will not know where he is. If you find out, he will be moved. He will be a stranger in his foster home, not a member of the family. He will be far away from his brothers and sisters, and his friends.

Meanwhile mom and dad must spend all kinds of money to defend themselves against the false allegations, and probably paying for sonny boy's foster care on top of that.

After explaining these consequences to the child, you must make him consider if he is willing to risk losing his family over his imagined suffering. This is no exaggeration, he is risking losing his family, possibly permanently. Once intervention has started, especially if it is instigated by the child, the family bond is severely damaged. It is difficult if not impossible to trust that child again. This is how devastating intervention can be.

You must also explain to him that you would fight the charge, which means you would be risking going to jail if convicted. Is this what he wants for his mom or dad? Make sure he understands that the courts are not always fair, and there are many innocent people in prison.

If, after all of this, he seems determined to pursue this course, I'd remove him from school and restrict his access to other children until his attitude genuinely improves. Some children will do anything to get control over their parents, and the agents of the state will help them do it. This can be done without letting on why you are doing it. Don't get into a battle of the wills with the child. Simply state that you're not happy with the school. It is, after all, the truth.

At this point, you might want to consider family counseling. This will serve several purposes. First, it will help resolve the problem that is causing the child to consider getting intervention. Many times our children won't share with us the things that are bothering them. A counselor of your choosing, can facilitate communication without violating your family values or integrity. Many times, the counselor can help the child understand that what the parents are doing is right, and that they do love and understand the child.

Once the communication is restored, many of the conflicts and problems will diminish or fade away. The restoration of communication depends on the honesty of the participants. It may take some time to get a recalcitrant child to open up and be honest. It will be easier to accomplish if the child is removed from the deceitful influence of the agents of the state. Keep him away from school, monitor his radio and television, limit his access to undesirable friends. Be persistent and loving. There is a lot at stake.

Another advantage of family counseling is that it can establish your credibility in the event of a trial. It will demonstrate that you attempted to resolve the problem in a rational and socially acceptable manner, thereby undermining any allegation of your reacting irrationally or emotionally.

Finally, you will have access to an expert witness who can verify your parenting skills as well as the state of mind and physical condition of the child during the time period the family was being counseled. A counselor, by law, is required to report suspected cases of child abuse. If the child didn't confess abuse to the counselor, then it seems more likely that the abuse didn't occur.

You must remember, if your child is considering making allegations of abuse, it is not because he doesn't love you. While children naturally want to get away with as much as possible, they clearly are relieved when parents put fair limits on them and enforce those limits. The state has played into the child's immature desire without consideration for what is best for the child. They don't protect children. They exploit children.

In order to get the most federal funding, they need the children to be removed from their homes. They don't care about the children, so they lie to them to get their cooperation. They abuse the trust of the child with this dishonesty. These mixed messages, one from the parents and one from the agents of the state, surely confuse the child. Being unwise and immature, they often make the wrong decision. Only you, the parent, can protect them from being exploited by the state.

CHAPTER 5

TEACH YOUR CHILDREN TO PROTECT YOUR FAMILY

"Education is a better safeguard of liberty than a standing army." Edward Everett

The need to teach your children to protect your family is no different from teaching them to stay away from strangers. And, after all, most of the agents of the state are strangers. In my opinion, they are more dangerous than strangers.

There is a great risk in depending on your children to protect your family. You have taught them to obey and trust their teachers and the police. But you have not taught them how these people can hurt them, or that they even would hurt them. On top of that, the teachers, counselors, and police claim to be protecting the children. Now you must teach your children to distrust these same figures of authority. Therein lies the risk.

It is appropriate, and even needful to trust the agents of the state. However, it is very difficult to teach a child when they should trust them and when not to. I believe most children will be unable to make the distinction on their own. Many times, when false allegations against the parents are prosecuted, the children recognize the betrayal by the agents of the state, and come to distrust, and even actively hate these authority figures. Then who can they turn to in their hour of genuine need?

Children cannot distinguish between what should be private and what isn't private. They cannot discern truth from falsehoods when it comes from authority figures. They are easily manipulated, and false suggestions are easily implanted into their minds.[19] They are eager to please adults, and will do so by whatever means are necessary.[20] This means that they will be inclined to agree with the social worker who presses for a falsehood just to make her happy, without understanding the consequences. Personally, I would avoid teaching my children to protect the family by keeping them out of all public and most private schools. The risk is too great. If this sounds too extreme, please remember, I'm speaking from experience. Mine and the experiences of many other parents who almowt universally wished they'd taken their children out of school.

Having said that, I'll plunge ahead.

According to a sheriff's investigator, statistically speaking, you have a greater chance of having your children removed from your home than you do of having your house burn down. This represents a great danger to you and your family. You need to recognize the danger signals before it is too late and intervene. Sometimes, unfortunately, your child will have to carry the ball.

You must impress upon your children from a young age that they absolutely must not divulge private family information to anyone outside of the family. An innocent remark, misinterpreted by a social worker, will trigger an investigation for child abuse. Agents of the state routinely misinterpret events. Therefore, nothing about the

---

[19]Ceci, Stephen J. (Cornell University) and Bruck, Maggie (McGill University). *The Suggestibility of the Child Witness: A Historical Review and Synthesis*

[20] *Families in Crisis* a report by the 1991-92 San Diego County Grand Jury.

family should be said to them. Nothing.

The counselors and teachers at school make themselves available to help students, encouraging them to talk about their problems. They practice their own brand of amateur psychology on your children, often presenting values and ideas that conflict with yours. To avoid this conflict, teach your children not to talk about personal problems with anyone at school. Those people are best equipped to help solve academic problems, not personal problems. Your child should only go to them for school-related issues.

If your child needs to talk to someone and they don't want to talk to you, arrange for them to talk to a trusted pastor, a professional family counselor, or a close family member. Make sure that the child's confidant shares your values. Encourage the child to be honest with his confidant. Reassure him that you don't want to invade his privacy but as his parent you are entitled to know what's bothering him, and that the confidant will help him share that with you when he's ready. Make sure this confidant works with both you the parent and the child.

Teach your children from a young age, not to exaggerate. Especially not to exaggerate incidents between family members when speaking to their friends or adults. This includes teachers, police, pastors, counselors, etc. They must understand that others will believe the exaggeration is the truth and it could get someone else into trouble.

Your children must never answer nosy or private questions about the family or family members on the phone or from anyone at the door. They must also never answer these questions when asked by a police officer, unless there is genuine abuse involved. They must never allow the police or social workers into the house, the same as any other stranger.

If you must keep your children in school, try to teach them to recognize profiling and that they must report any such profiling to you immediately. What is profiling? These are often tests administered under the guise of academic assessments which reveal information about your home life, lifestyle, beliefs, and other private information. The information gathered is used to create a profile of you and your family. This profile is used to target families whose values differ from society's desired values.

What the children should be alert for are questions about family members, religious beliefs, discipline styles, size of household, or anything else that does not relate to an academic subject. These questions should not be answered.

As your children get older, they will be subjected to values clarification or dialectic thinking. Values clarification involves taking tests or having group sessions to resolve a particular moral problem that allegedly has no right or wrong answer. For example: You are in a lifeboat with seven other people, a preacher, an actress, a scientist, a mother, a doctor, a sailor, and a banker. You only have enough food and water for seven people. You decide who must die so the rest can live. This is presented as acceptable; to determine which innocent person is to be sacrificed so that the greater good may be served. What your child will fail to understand is that this scenario is morally wrong, and he should not participate in making that decision. If he does resist, he will be compelled by the teacher to participate or risk a failing grade. This type of exercise is designed to undermine the Biblical values instilled by parents, and to socialize the child to the moral relativity practiced by society as a whole.

Free discussion or group sessions are especially

effective for getting a child to reveal personal information about himself. There was in incident in Colorado, where a high school class was taken on a secret field trip on a Saturday. As the students got off of the bus, they were told to take as many sheets as they thought they would need from the roll of toilet paper offered. They were not told what they would need it for. Some students took a single sheet. Some took a whole wad. The group was assembled into a circle. Each student was then instructed to stand up in front of the group and tell one bad thing about themselves for each sheet of toilet paper they took. This was done without the parents knowledge, and it was a mandatory requirement for graduation.

This again falls into the realm of revealing personal, private information. This is forwarded to the counselors and becomes a part of the child's record. If this record is computerized, it is likely to be forwarded to a national database, and be available to anyone who has access to that database. It is a given, as the parent, you will not be allowed access to that database. If nobody even acknowledges the existence of this data base, nobody can successfully file a freedom of information request. The information compiled can also be used to prosecute the parent. Your children should not participate in these type of events.

They should also watch out for tests that have subjective answers such as: I agree strongly, I agree, I disagree, I disagree strongly. Any test that has questions or answers with the word "I," or relates to personal feelings and/or actions is highly suspect and should not be answered by your child. Additionally, many times, children will be instructed to keep certain tests and projects secret from the parents. This is a huge red flag, and your children should be taught not to participate and to inform you of this immediately in all cases involving keeping secrets from the parents. If you try to obtain a copy of the questionable test or project in question, it is unlikely the school will honor your demand. It would reveal their illegal actions and put them at risk of a lawsuit.

The same goes for dialectic thinking. This is the process of examining the truth or validity of a theory or opinion by question and answer or argument. This process is used to arrive at a group consensus regarding moral and personal issues. The outcome is predetermined and the direction of the process is carefully guided by the facilitator. This process teaches the children to "be their own person." Being such, they don't have to follow their parents' rules or respect their values and authority. Rather than right and wrong being absolute, it is determined by the majority vote of the group. Peer pressure is used by the facilitator, often their own teacher, to change your child's values. The facilitator will react favorably to the response suggested by the children that corresponds with the desired response. The facilitator then subtly encourages the children who have responded "correctly" to put pressure on the dissenting children to conform. Already, homosexuality is approved of and endorsed by the schools, and children who are taught by their parents that it is wrong, have learned to hide that opinion from their peers and teachers. If the ploy is successful, it can put the parent who spanks at risk of prosecution, instigated by the child.

The problem is that there are so many devious and subtle tactics being used that it is extremely difficult to teach your child what to look for. It's extremely hard to recognize it even as an adult.

You will have to make the decision whether you teach your child to challenge these tactics or simply refuse to comply. Either way, he will be subjected to extreme pressure to comply, and he may not be able to handle it. He will be frightened and intimidated, and that's a tough position for a child to be in. He will probably be denied the right to call you, because the school doesn't want you there to protect him from what they are doing. They will keep him there and coerce him to change his mind, or force him to comply.

Can this be true? It sounds unbelievable, but it happens. On March 19, 1996 in East Stroudsburg, Pennsylvania, 59 eleven year old girls were herded into J.T. Lambert Intermediate School's medical office and forced to undress and submit to a genital examination administered by a doctor at the school's direction. It is questionable whether all parents were notified in advance of this examination. Any letters which explicitly denied permission for the school to conduct medical exams have "disappeared."

The girls were frightened and embarrassed. Many said their parents would object and wanted to call their parents. The school refused to let them call. The exams were performed without sheets or gowns to cover the girls' nakedness. These young girls were traumatized and their parents outraged. This was government sanctioned sexual abuse, sponsored by the school. Are your children really safe in school?

As you can see, even if your children resist, the school can force them to comply with their demands. This places your dear child at risk of emotional trauma or injury. What is done, cannot be undone. This is why prevention is so important. Is the risk to your child worth it for your convenience, so both parents can work outside the home? And aren't you as much to blame as the perpetrators of the violations of privacy and parental authority by allowing your child to be placed in a situation where he could be exposed to such abuses?

Let's suppose your child has been able to resist the efforts to recondition his mind. Let's further suppose he is being questioned about you allegedly abusing him or his siblings. The most important thing for your child to remember is to never answer any questions about it unless he really has been abused. I instructed my son to simply say, "I don't want to answer any questions without my parents here." Under the Privacy Act of 1974, once a child invokes this act by name, he cannot be questioned without his parents present. But could he remember to invoke it? It is an easy line to memorize and they can't go wrong when they say that, and only that. They cannot even give any 'yes' or 'no' answers to anything. You must understand that there will be many people trying to get an answer out of him; principal, teacher, counselor, social worker, police and more. It will be very scary for this child. No one will be on his side, no one will let him call his parents if they can possibly prevent it. They will exert all the authority they can muster to make him answer.

These agents of the state will lie, promising him you (the parents) won't get into trouble, promising him safety and help, whether he needs it or not. They will say they cannot get a hold of you. They'll try to convince him he's in danger. They'll promise to see to it that you get help. They will lie.

They may try to remove him forcibly from school and into the custody of the police or social services. If he doesn't want to be taken out his home, he should say so. He should say, "I'm not in any danger, I want to go home." He should tell it to the social worker, the police, the foster parents, the judge, whomever he can. You have to make the decision about how you want your child to react, if you want him to make a public display of resisting or not. Either way, he can claim he's being kidnaped, or being taken against his will. This action alone is likely to be useless other than to establish an unwarranted action by the agents of the state.

He may be appointed a Guardian ad Litem, who is usually a lawyer and is supposed to protect the child's interest. Some areas are lax about this requirement. He can demand to speak to the Guardian ad Litem and reassert his demand to go home. The GAL is supposed to be an advocate for the child, but often they are merely a prop for the state. He can ask the Guardian ad Litem or his foster parents to contact his pastor for him. The pastor can then become an advocate for the child against a corrupt system. He can help the child convince the court that the child never was in any danger.

Your child should not misbehave in his foster home. Children who are uncontrollable are often drugged to calm them down. Even worse, sometimes, they are taken to juvenile detention and locked up with juvenile criminals. Either option is bad for the child, so his good behavior will prevent such abuses.

He should be instructed not to take any medicines or pills offered by strangers, including unknown doctors and foster parents. He should demand that only his personal physician administer any medications. This can forestall abuses by the system in their efforts to control him, and bring another advocate for the child into the system. Many good family physicians are disgusted at the abuses by the system and would be more than willing to prevent abuses against their patient. Is your family doctor one of the good ones? It is best to find out before something goes wrong.

Your child should not submit to any medical exam except with his family doctor. He can clearly state, to the strange doctor and the agents of the state, "I want my own doctor." If they deny him, you may have grounds for a lawsuit against the doctor. A reputable doctor should be very reluctant to examine an obviously healthy but unwilling patient, especially without the child's parents present.

There is a new phenomenon out there, unified centers for sexual assault and child abuse investigations. These are one-stop centers with medical facilities, counselors, and investigators, designed to simplify the collection of evidence and data. The victim is processed by agents of the state at every step. Children are also processed, securely behind closed doors, and often without a genuine advocate. They will be examined by strange doctors and questioned by police psychologists. Their testimony will be twisted and used against you. Under the color of law, and abusing their position of authority over the child, they will strip search your child and photograph your child's naked body. They will ask him leading questions to facilitate their case against you. They are not interested in the truth. They are on a witch hunt.

Most times, the child will never see the judge. It often happens that the child's demands are never even presented to the judge. Especially if the child has recanted his story. The judge never knows about this, or if he does, it is presented in a very slanted way and discounted by the social workers. Perhaps your child could write a personal letter to the judge, and mail it directly to him, and send a copy to the clerk of court to become a part of the record. I don't know of anyone who has tried this, but since everyone tries so hard to keep the child away from the judge, it just might work. There's no reason that you cannot file documents into the court record on your own and your child's behalf. It's not against the law and it brings the evidence that is favorable to your case to the attention of the judge. It certainly is a way to get around the stone wall erected by the agents of the state. Affidavits are especially effective in other types of cases, why not this?

If your child does get to see his pastor or the judge, make sure he continues to say he was safe at home, and that he wants to go home. He should also tell them if he was forcibly taken, or if he was drugged against his will or forced to submit to an unwanted physical examination. He should be sure to tell the judge and the pastor, and the Guardian ad Litem if he is in danger or actually suffering abuse in his foster home or group home. Again, he must not exaggerate or lie about that. If it accomplishes nothing else, it will at least establish for the record that everything was done against the child's best interests. And that is supposed to be the ultimate measure these days, isn't it?

There is a recurring, contradictory theme played by the agents of the state. If a child is in the custody of the state, and claims he was abused while in their custody, they will insist there is no validity to his claim. If he made a false accusation and recanted, they will believe in the original accusation, discount the recanted story, and deny the abuse in the foster home. They've got it all backwards, they believe the lies and don't believe the truth. Your child is not safe in the custody of the state.

With the new education legislation being passed, you will find that the schools are becoming one-stop community centers covering medical, psychological, social, vocational, and community issues. In an obscene effort to gain absolute control over the child and his family, many services will be offered for "free." The only cost will be the demise of the family who partakes. Keep a skeptical eye on any school program that deals with anything other than "reading, writing, and 'rithmatic."

This has been an ugly chapter. Full of bad things children must watch out for. In all honesty, I sincerely doubt you can get your child to effectively assert his rights, and the agents of the state are counting on that fact. Protecting his rights is your job, and it starts with you not putting him into a position where he would be forced to assert them or relinquish them. This is an adult battle, and your child cannot fight it. He lacks the credibility and authority of an adult, and he lacks the clout to make them comply. If you control his environment, you control his safety. Let him out of your control, and he's on his own. Is he ready for that yet? Are you?

CHAPTER 6

SOCIAL SERVICES AT YOUR DOOR

"There's a growing army of families that are willing to fight for the rights of families and not just roll over and play dead every time some person who's wearing a gun or a badge or a social worker's uni(form) says 'You gotta do this because we're from the government. We're here to help you'." Scott Somerville, Lawyer, Home School Legal Defense Association.

Up until now, we have been dealing with situations that are out of your control regarding Social Services intervention. I have said more than once that it is best to keep the child out of public school. In this chapter, you will learn why.

The most important rule is this: "Fight over the doorknob, not the child." The battle for your children is a tug-of-war with the child in the middle. However, you cannot have this tug-of-war if the social worker cannot get her hands on the child.

She can get her hands on the child if the child is in public school. It's easy. School officials just hand sonny boy over, no questions asked. She cannot get her grubby hands on your children if you control their environment and her access to them. The key here is to completely deny her any access to your children. Once she has them in custody, it's nearly impossible to get them back on your terms. You'll find they want to continue to intervene (read: interfere) in your life, and you will no longer be the authority in your home. They will control you.

Your best friend will be your video camera. If you don't have one, then use an audio tape recorder. Record *every single encounter* you have with agents of the state, and keep these recordings in a safe place. Make duplicates if possible. In Colorado, where I live, it is legal to secretly record a conversation if one party to the conversation has knowledge of the recording. If you can record secretly in your state, you get to decide if you want to divulge the fact that you are recording or not. I don't think it makes much difference other than to intimidate the agent of the state and make them a little more circumspect in what they say and do.

Even if the police are at your door, record everything. I have had officers refuse to allow the recording, so I terminate the interview immediately. You are entitled to your own record of every proceeding, including in court. If someone, including a judge, orders you to turn off the recorder, simply ask, "Are you denying me my right to have my own record of these proceedings?" It is unlikely they will deny you your rights. Doing so gives you cause for a lawsuit against them. I have seen court transcripts which do not accurately reflect what was actually said in the courtroom. Do you want to risk your freedom on such inaccuracies?

If you have a social worker standing at your front door, demanding to be let in, you just say no. That's right. Don't let her in. You are within your rights and the law to refuse entrance to her. Once you do, you have relinquished all your rights, and you cannot reassert them again later. This is the one most important thing you will do. Do not permit anyone to step a single foot in your house without a warrant. You should open your door, step outside and *close the door tightly behind you.* Block the access to the door with your body.

Then, I go even one step further, I inform her that she is trespassing and demand that she leave my property immediately. I don't listen to or answer any of her questions. I don't care about her questions, I only care about my issue; that she is trespassing. Most social workers don't encounter this kind of resistance. They are used to being able to bully and bluff their way into people's homes. Then they have complete control over you, because you've given it to them on a silver platter.

The social worker will sputter and fume and try to threaten you with removal of your children. Are you scared yet? No doubt you are trembling. I've been there, and I was mad and scared. Just smile and remind her that she is trespassing, and you will be forced to call the police if she doesn't leave immediately. If you want, you can tell her you understand her concern, but that it is unwarranted. Then go into your house and lock the door behind you. She'll probably leave. If she doesn't leave, call the police and report a trespasser. This complaint will not go over well with her boss. Be warned. You have really angered her. If at all possible, she'll be back. She may also try to get your neighbors to make false accusations. She'll try every dirty trick in the book. If you are smart, she'll only be digging her own grave. Document everything.

The social worker may claim she has a warrant. Demand to see it. She'll say she can get one. She lied. She doesn't have one. Social services cannot legally serve a warrant. A warrant must be served by an officer of the law.

What if the police are present with her? Often, social workers will use uniformed officers, wearing badges and guns, to intimidate parents under the color of law, and get you to open the door and let them in. You must understand, the police are not your friends, the social worker is not your friend. They will not protect your rights. They will violate your rights. You must assert your rights yourself. One of these rights is that you do not have to let anyone into your home without a warrant.

Would you recognize one if you saw it? A warrant

must be signed by a judge, with a sworn affidavit attached and signed under penalty of perjury by the person swearing to the information contained in the affidavit. No affidavit, no valid warrant. Additionally, the warrant must state the specific items to be searched for. If they are looking for your children, they cannot search in dresser drawers, because it is impossible for your children to be inside them. They'll try to do it anyway. Just be sure you're video taping everything.

Chances are there is no warrant. In order for a warrant to be issued, there must be probable cause. This means they must have some evidence to back up their claim, meaning someone has submitted evidence that you abused your child.

If the boys in blue are with the social worker demanding to be let in, get your tape recorder, go outside and close the door behind you. Ask politely if they have a warrant. If not, get the officer's names and badge numbers, then tell them they are trespassing and ask them to leave. They may ask you your name or ask for other information. Don't answer anything. Ask again if they have a warrant. If they don't have one, demand that they leave your property. By law, they must leave. Usually they will.

Suppose they don't have a warrant but they claim the child is in imminent danger and they must remove him for his own safety? This is a legally valid reason to remove the child from the home. It is often used as an excuse to remove a child from an undesirable home if a warrant cannot be obtained. You have a lot more power to prevent them from taking your child under these circumstances.

They may threaten to break the door down to obtain your child. Inform them you are recording everything and ask politely for proof that the child is in imminent danger. Remind them that they will have to prove imminent danger in court, too. They must state specifically what the danger is, and why they believe the danger exists. What you really want to do is get them to admit that the child is not in imminent danger on your tape. Ask them to explain what they mean, question everything they say. Pretend you are really stupid, and they have to make you understand. Don't answer any of their questions. Meanwhile, get your trusted advocates (family, friends, pastor, etc.) over to vouch for you and be your witnesses. Have them bring their recorders and video cameras, too.

If you open your door to meet them outside, they may try to push past you into the house. I prefer to communicate through an open window near the door. This makes it more difficult for them to take you down and confiscate your recording equipment. They don't like being recorded, so the more recording equipment you have recording, the better it will be for you. Make sure you are video taping them through the window, and make sure they know it.

Your heart will be racing, and you'll be shaking from the adrenaline that is flooding your body. You must be rational. This is not the time for knee-jerk reactions. Speak calmly but firmly. Make your movements slow and deliberate, keep your hands visible at all times so they don't have any excuse to get rough with you. Your knowledge of the law and your rights will be absolutely necessary if you are going to protect your family. Do not inadvertently surrender any of your rights. Answering a single question could possibly be that surrender. A good tactic is to always answer their question with a question of your own.

At this point you may have to prove that your child is not in imminent danger. Offer to let them see the children through a window or open door. If they view the children through an open door, the agents of the government and the children must each be standing well back, away from the door; agents outside, children inside. Get them to admit on your tape the children do not appear to be in danger or injured.

Once they see the children are not in imminent danger, politely but firmly demand that the agents of the state leave your property.

They may demand to examine the children for bruises or other injury. Do not allow this. If it looks like they won't relent, offer to take the child to your family doctor to be examined. This is a reasonable request which should allay any of their fears. They can hardly refuse this condition and maintain credibility.

If they agree, ask them to leave your property. You may have to go directly to the doctor to satisfy the agents of the state, or they may accept your offer to have them examined sometime that same day. Do not let the agents of the state take your children to the doctor. You load the children into your car, and you take them to your family doctor. Inform the agents of the state that the doctor will provide them with an affidavit of his findings within a day or two. Hopefully they won't accompany you.

If they do follow you, don't let your children out of your grasp for an instant. You could also have your trusted advocates assist you in forming a protective cordon around your children. They will be less inclined to violate your rights or make any unreasonable moves with lots of witnesses around.

Inform your doctor that you are aware of his legal obligation to report child abuse and you have no intention of preventing him from doing his duty. However, you have not abused your child and you just want him to verify that fact to get these rabid people off of your back.

If he's inclined to permit an interview by the agents of the state, remind him he may violate a doctor/patient confidence if he answers too many questions. He should simply state whether or not he found clear evidence of abuse. There are many instances of normal childhood injuries that could be "consistent with abuse" but are not caused by abuse. Make sure your doctor understands that he must find clear and convincing evidence of abuse. You should be present while he speaks with them, with your trusty tape machine recording.

With you in the room, have the doctor examine the kiddies for evidence of abuse. The agents of the state are not permitted to witness this examination. Yes, you want at least an audio tape of this, too. The doctor can then prepare an affidavit stating his findings about abuse. Make sure he sends a copy of that affidavit to you, too.

It is important that you trust your family doctor. Many ordinary childhood accidents can be construed as abuse by a suspicious and twisted mind. If you've known your doctor for a while, and he's seen your children over the years, he can tell if they are in an abusive home or not. He can be a valuable advocate.

You can also offer to have the social worker call your pastor or family counselor and confirm that the children are in no danger from you. She probably won't. She's not interested in that kind of evidence.

Offer her a sworn affidavit from these professionals, and get all these offers on tape, along with her responses. You are gathering valuable evidence just in case you need it. Keep duplicates to file with the court.

They may still insist on taking the child, citing imminent danger. Maybe because they have to wait for the doctor's affidavit, or maybe someone just has it in for you. They are mandated by law to try and keep the family together, but that doesn't mean they'll actually follow the law. Since they insist on removing the child, you can offer to have the child placed in a prearranged safe home of your choosing. The law further states that if they cannot keep the family together, they must try to find a relative to place the child with. If they agree to that, you must abide by their rules regarding visitation with your children. You can at least take some comfort in the fact that the children will be with family, and your family can aid in their protection against the agents of the state.

Make sure the relatives you have chosen to foster your children will not just hand the children over to the agents of the state. They must understand the seriousness of their responsibility regarding your children while they are caring for them.

Some social services agencies claim to want to respect the family's values and are striving to place children in like-minded foster homes. They are even recruiting foster families from churches, and you might be able to get them to put your children in a foster family from your church. Lots of luck.

A WARRANT

If the police have a warrant, you must let them in. Call your lawyer immediately. If you have decided to forego the lawyer, you need to get someone you trust to represent the child during the questioning, possibly your pastor or family counselor. I would also get as many witnesses over to my house as quickly as possible. You'll need someone to vouch for you. Call your pastor, your family counselor, close friends, your lawyer, and family members. These will be your trusted advocates.

By all means, do not allow the agents of the state to interrogate your children privately. They may want to take the child to a bedroom and start asking leading questions or even strip search him. There will only be the interrogator's word for what was said and witnessed; these interrogations are not generally recorded. You or your lawyer should be allowed to set up the terms of the interrogation. You must have someone present at this questioning to insure that the child is not being misled or confused. If you have all of these demands on your tape, and they deny them, you have grounds for a lawsuit against every individual who violated your child's and your rights.

If they take the child, find out where the child will be questioned and have your representative present at that questioning. If your lawyer cannot make it, he should be able to send someone to take his place. Insist that all interrogations be videotaped.

There's little you can do to prevent them from taking the child if they have a warrant. The good news is that they usually don't have warrants except for very obvious cases of abuse and neglect. If you have not abused your child, it is unlikely they can obtain a warrant.

They may also neglect to inform you of the mandatory hearing. When a child is forcibly removed from a home, you are entitled to a hearing within a specific time frame, somewhere between 24 and 72 hours depending on what state you live in. If they don't inform you and you don't know, they may just neglect to have the hearing, or have it without you. Laws vary from state to state. Find out what your laws are, and show up in court with volumes of proof of your child's safety and demand his immediate return to your custody. Bring witnesses and all your trusted advocates. Bring the child's medical records. Bring sworn affidavits from people who cannot make it in person.

Affidavits are valuable evidence. Social services and the court are making the presumption that you are a child abuser. The only way to rebut a presumption is with evidence. It is amazing how many attorneys and accused parents will not rebut this most basic presumption of the court. According to the rules of evidence, an affidavit, sworn under the penalty of perjury, made by a person who has first hand knowledge of the facts, and being competent to testify, is evidence that controverts the presumption. The agents of the state must then produce their own evidence to prove yours wrong. They rarely can. You must have your ducks in a row, and now is the time to line them up.

You have the legal right to file anything related to your case in the court record. The judge is required by law to read what's in the file. You don't need your lawyer's help or approval to do this, either. This circumvents the possibility that the judge would disallow something you wanted admitted as evidence.

Flood that courtroom with proof of your exceptional parenting skills and good character. If the judge tries to disallow your evidence and it violates your rights, you can file a lawsuit against him. Have the Title 42 lawsuit all filled out with his, and all the other violators of your civil rights, names. You are entitled as a constitutional right to submit any evidence that rebuts the evidence submitted by social services. Make sure he understands that you know your rights, and are willing to fight for them. You might find the judge more willing to be fair and impartial.

Do not accept any conditions on the return of your child. If you haven't abused your child, you haven't done anything wrong, no matter what other people say. If you've done nothing wrong, why should you agree to their conditions? It is morally wrong to accept punishment and/or conditions if you have done nothing wrong.

They may want to demand social services visitations, or that you attend parenting classes, or some other invasive thing. Do not agree to conditions. Demand that they prove the charges or release your child to your custody, or you will file your Title 42 lawsuit in Federal Court as soon as you are done in this court.

I have seen, over and over again, parents who are at the mercy of social services, who do not, will not, or are too scared to fight the way I describe in this chapter. They always lose against social services. Always. Many times, they place unwarranted hope on the capricious whim of a social worker and actually come to believe that maybe they deserved to have this horrible intervention and child snatching happen to them.

Most social workers are masters of manipulation. I've already told you how they manipulate children, but they also deceive and manipulate adults. They mastered the arts of gentle innuendos and vague promises, but try to get them to commit to anything, and they'll have you running in circles chasing your own shadow. They can calm an irate parent and tell him tricky lies until he's rolling over and licking their feet, willing to agree to *just one more little condition* in order to get his children back. He's already forgotten all the other conditions he agreed to that they reneged on. They will make him argue about anything and everything except his important issue, that being the return of his children. He will have forgotten that his rights were violated and his children kidnaped. He's forgotten that he's been violated and treated like a criminal without a shred of evidence. He's forgotten that his job, his marriage, and everything he's worked for is at risk.

By the time his meeting is over, he is no better off than when he walked in, but he feels better about it. Until he gets back home, that is. And the social worker has gathered another batch of evidence to use against him because *he talked his mouth off* trying to convince them of his innocence. What you say never changes their minds.

You must learn to listen. Make your demands and listen for their response. Do not fill the uncomfortable silences with ramblings and explanations. This will be the hardest thing to do, but it is so simple that you can't go wrong. Do not give them any information. You should only speak to ask questions and make demands.

I must make one qualification; not all social workers are evil. But most often, the good ones are so disgusted by what they see and what they must do, that they don't stay around very long.

One thing is certain, nobody can convince anyone of the abuses perpetrated under the name of child protection until it happens to them or someone they know. This book is not intended to educate the nonbelievers. They'll be believers soon enough. Hopefully it won't be too late.

REFUSE TO COOPERATE WITH SOCIAL SERVICES

Now that the investigation has been initiated, you must be careful of your every word. You will probably be notified of the social worker's desire to interview you, whether they have custody of your children or not. If you show up for the interview, you can expect to be led down the primrose path.

The social worker will portray a false impression of wanting to help. She will be very concerned about your children and about you. She will ask questions about the incident being investigated, wanting your side of the story. She is gathering evidence to use against you. This evidence will be twisted and distorted in court to present the most awful impression of you as a person and a parent. Don't forget, she thinks you are the slime of the earth, a disgusting child abuser who doesn't deserve to have children. Or if she's feeling charitable, you are merely misguided or old-fashioned and must be reeducated to her way of thinking.

I firmly believe that my husband and I did not end up in family court (or civil court) because we refused to speak with the social worker or the police. This denied them any evidence that they could distort or tamper with to institute their favorite type or proceeding - Dependency and Neglect (D&N). With civil cases, as D&N, they can keep you dangling and dancing to their tune forever, as well as keep your children in custody forever. You must do your best to stay out of family court. It is your best hope.

To accomplish this, you should just refuse to cooperate with their investigation. Don't go to interviews, don't answer questions, don't let anyone into your house. Refuse their calls. Say nothing at all. Follow up every contact with the agents of the state with a registered/certified letter detailing the content of the conversation. Send this to the relevant agent of the state using registered mail. Save all return receipts along with copies of the letters. It should say something about the date and time of the conversation, what was said and by whom, and give them ten days to reply in writing if they dispute your understanding of the conversation. No reply, no dispute.

If they get your cooperation, they will jerk you around like a puppet on a string. They know you want your children back and you'll do anything to get them back. Each time you meet one of their demands, they'll renege on their promises to you and make another demand for you to meet. It is impossible to satisfy them. Even if you jump through all their hoops, it will never be good enough for them. It's a no-win situation.

It's a slick system. During the assessment process, you will deny that you are an abuser. They will determine that you are in denial and therefore you shouldn't get your children back. In an effort to please them and get your children back, you falsely admit abuse. Now you are unfit. Do you see how it works? You can't win. So you simply must not play their game. It's rigged against parents.

Meanwhile they are gathering volumes of evidence, surrendered by you voluntarily. This will be used against you, guaranteed. If they can't gather this evidence, they can't use it can they? The worst they can say is that you refused to cooperate with the investigation. Is that any worse than saying you are an abuser or in denial? I don't think so.

They will also try these tactics against you if they don't have your children. They want to suck you into the system so they can snatch your children based on the evidence you give them.

It is not in your best interest to cooperate with social services. You cannot win. Let them run around in circles trying to get you into the system, but stand firm. Give them nothing to work with. Keep your mouth shut. It's the best tactic to use.

If they don't have your children yet, make it impossible for them to get them. Take your children out of school. All social services has to do is ask the school to relinquish custody of your child, and it's that easy, the child is turned over. No questions asked. Social services loves the school system.

I've heard social workers state that if they were under investigation for child abuse, they'd move out of the state. Does that instill confidence in the child protection system? These insiders know they cannot get fair treatment at the hands of their colleagues, so they'd run. One even admitted that she'd leave everything behind and get out that very night. Comforting thought.

Many of us are unwilling to acknowledge the severity of what's at stake, and moving may not be a viable solution. In cases where there is probable cause of abuse, moving may even be illegal.

You might think you can send the children to a distant relative while you straighten things out. This will deny the state access to the children. Their inability to collect evidence will seriously weaken their case. However, you may be accused of hiding the children and face criminal charges for hiding them and refusing to divulge their whereabouts.

In my case, Jacob was in a residential treatment facility. I informed the staff that if they divulged his location, I'd sue them. They naturally said they were mandated to report abuse. I told them I knew that, but if they reported it, they had better be sure that Jacob was actually abused. Then, I told social services he was in a safe place that was none of their business. They couldn't find him, but even with their witness gone, they refused to drop the case. I refused all of their calls.

When the trial came, they had little evidence, and looked positively foolish. The only evidence they did have was given to them by my own hand before I knew what they were doing and how they operated. I foolishly showed the police the martinet and they snatched it out of my hand and kept it for the trial. They never would have gotten it if I had refused to let them in my house that one time and refused to speak to them. What more proof does anyone need not to cooperate with the agents of the state?

I did face contempt charges, but we had a fair judge, and she refused to find me in contempt because I honestly did not know Jacob's whereabouts by the time the trial occurred. If I had known his whereabouts, I would have been jailed for refusing to divulge his location. Removing your children from their jurisdiction is risky, and it can backfire on you, unless you know what you are doing.

I believe it is better to keep them with you. It gives you complete control over their environment. If you want the children moved out of the jurisdiction, you should probably move the entire family. Be forewarned though, they can track you through the children's schools, and through your social security number. That means jobs, credit purchases and bank accounts. Unless you have established that the child has not been abused, and gotten them to acknowledge that, you could be guilty of criminal behavior by running. You might be better off staying and fighting, and beating them into the ground legally.

It probably seems strange that you can legally refuse to cooperate with social services. They are such a powerful agency. At least that's what they want you to believe.

In truth, social services has little actual statutory authority and power. This was demonstrated earlier, when you learned that social services cannot issue a warrant, cannot enter your home without permission, and cannot simply whisk your children away without cause unless you let them.

The child protection agencies operate on ignorance and intimidation. They are able to intimidate ignorant parents and bully them into complying with their demands by lying to them about the law and their authority. They also operate on the "possession is 90% of the law" principle. If they have your children, they have the control. They create their own version of a hostage crisis, with your children as hostages. The good news is that they usually require your cooperation to get your children. Without that, they can initiate very little on their own except in the case of clear evidence of abuse. It's very simple to refuse to cooperate and deny them their hostages.

What they can do is take reports of accusations and investigate those reports. They must have proof to bring before the court in order to obtain a court order to take the children. This is why few court orders are issued. So they must lie to get your cooperation. They depend on your voluntary surrender of the children.

You must know the law to protect yourself, because social workers don't give a hoot about the law. They'll use the police to project a false image of legality behind their actions. What is worse, these sorry specimens of law enforcement let themselves be used to intimidate and coerce law-abiding parents. It's disgusting.

Since social workers have little actual authority and power under the law, they are counting on your shame and embarrassment to maintain their tyranny through secrecy. Most people won't talk about what happened to them, so this tyranny continues. They'll threaten to expose your dirty secret if you don't cooperate. You need to call their bluff. If you aren't abusive, you have no dirty secret to expose.

They have another wonderful scam; the fake subpoena routine. If you are refusing to cooperate, they may try to bring you to the courthouse for your refusal to cooperate. There are documented cases where a social worker, faced with uncooperative parents, got a court lackey like an intake officer to fill out fake subpoenas. These subpoenas name the parents and/or the children, and order them to appear at a specified time and place at the courthouse. It says right on the subpoena "Failure to comply with this subpoena may result in a fine or being jailed for contempt of court." These subpoenas are signed by the clerk of court and delivered by an armed, uniformed police officer who threatens to arrest the parents if they do not appear at the appointed time and place.

Since these subpoenas are not issued in relation to a specific court case or any statute, and the court has no jurisdiction and asserts no jurisdiction over the case whatsoever, these subpoenas are completely bogus. Agents of the government do this just because it makes people come in. This is another example of social services using the color of law to commit fraud and get the parents to cooperate.

They do this because they can't figure out any other way to talk to the children. They can't get a warrant because they don't have probable cause. They also can't file a petition to initiate a case, because that also requires probable cause. If they can't talk to the children because they aren't going to school, so they can't get their evidence. Therefore, they have no case. The court should not support their illegal actions against you. There must be probable cause to force you to comply with their demands.

If you get a subpoena, either you or your lawyer should be able to validate its authenticity before you appear. If it is bogus, you are not required to appear. You can usually get the clerk of court to confirm the validity of a subpoena with a phone call. It might be helpful to give her a kind and gentle reminder of her personal liability (for acting outside the legitimate authority of her office) if she misrepresents the subpoena to you.

Asserting your rights is not easy. It requires extensive knowledge and great courage to defy counterfeit authority, especially when you are scared silly that you'll lose your children. Arm yourself with the knowledge of the law, and demand that the agents of the state comply fully with the law.

CHAPTER 7

NOT GUILTY!

"The only thing necessary for evil to triumph is for good men to do nothing." Edmund Burke 1729-1797

What if you are charged? Are you guilty of abusing your children? Statistics indicate that anywhere between 65% and 90% of people charged with child abuse have been falsely charged. The vast majority of these people, through threats, duress and coercion, will submit to an onerous plea bargain. Very few people actually fight the charges.

It's a shame, because according to a Douglas County, Colorado sheriff investigator, juries on child abuse cases rarely convict. It has been universally proven that those who cooperate with social services are the ones who suffer. Those who stand up and fight for their rights overwhelmingly win. As an added bonus, social services will think twice about intervening with the fighters again.

If you are not an abusive parent, you should stand up for your rights against this corrupt system. If you do not fight for your rights, you will lose them for yourself and for the other parents who follow you, and for your children when they become parents. If more people would stand up against the corrupt child protection system, fewer people would have to.

There are many ramifications to accepting a plea bargain. Many are hidden. Many will not be manifest until some time in the future. It is certain that for every person who accepts an unjustified plea bargain, he condemns more parents to suffer the same injustices.

Unfortunately, all those parents who have accepted a plea bargain in the past, are now no longer allowed to own a gun. It is clearly unconstitutional that such a ban can be made retroactive, but until somebody fights it we are stuck with complying with this bad law or with disobeying it. Keep this in mind if you are considering accepting a plea bargain. For your crime of domestic violence, you will be forever denied the right to keep and bear firearms. Yes, friends, spanking has become defacto domestic violence.

You may be advised that the record will be expunged upon your satisfactory completion of the terms of the plea bargain. Assuming that you can complete the terms, you need to know that the record is never expunged. I recently attended the trial of a juror, who was charged with contempt of court for her vote during jury deliberations. She had a previous plea bargain arrangement with the promise that her record would be expunged. It wasn't. In fact, it was used against her during her trial twelve years after the fact. A plea bargain is forever a part of your history.

Many lawyers will advise the accused parent to accept the plea bargain because it will be cheaper and easier. You must remember that lawyers are part of the system, with an oath to the bar that supersedes any obligation they have toward you, the client. Lawyers with integrity are rare. Pete and Jane in Colorado believed it when three different lawyers told them it would be cheaper to accept the plea bargain, so they accepted. They found out that the cost of state intervention is not measured only in dollars. They deeply regret their decision.

They were ordered into therapy, which ended up costing more than fighting the case would have cost. The therapist finally admitted they didn't belong in therapy; there was nothing wrong with them. They are required to get rid of their guns. Social services pried into every aspect of their life for more than two years.

Their children are uncontrollable because Pete and Jane are terrified to punish their children. Their children know how to turn mom and dad in for child abuse. They lost their home and both lost parents lost their jobs. All over a spanking.

If he had to do it over again, Pete bitterly vows he would fight the charges. He'd rather risk going to jail on a conviction than live under the terms of the plea bargain. He harbors a deep anger toward the government and its agents who destroyed his family and violated his rights. This deep wound may never heal.

Spanking is legal in every state. In fact, many states allow the schools to administer corporal punishment. Social workers know this but they just don't care. They personally don't like spanking and they have the means to make your life miserable if you do spank.

Their goal is to get the court involved somehow, so they can "force treatment" on parents who employ corporal punishment. This treatment is according to their values and on their terms. Colorado has six pilot Perpetrator Profile and Intervention programs which classify low, mid, and high risk offenders. Parents who strike their children, even just to spank, are classified are "mid-risk" offenders. As such, they are considered likely to repeat their "offense." The state wants to get these people to change their pattern of behavior. They are doing this with a three pronged attack by using the criminal justice system, social action, and offender's therapy. Once spanking has been established as abuse, they will attack other discipline methods until parents are powerless. Your state probably has the same type of program.

The only way you can avoid being caught up in this unholy web is to fight the charges and win. But it takes great courage to wage a fight against a corrupt child protection agency in an equally corrupt court system. Many people who don't think they have that kind of courage should ask themselves if they have the strength to endure the tyrannical terms of a plea bargain, and are willing to bow to the demands of a spoiled brat. They should ask themselves if they want their children to be subjected to even greater horrors by the state when they become parents. The ratchet effect of unreasonable government intervention can only be reversed when multitudes of parents take a stand and create enough of a public outcry to force the issue on all fronts.

PLEA BARGAIN

Plea bargains vary, but almost all of them involve obscene intrusions into your private life by the agents of the state. You will be required to attend therapy sessions until you repent of the sin of spanking your children (or yelling, or any other vague, state-sanctioned 'sins') and promise to never do it again. Your children will be instructed to turn you in if you spank them, and then you could go straight to jail without even having a trial. You will no longer be the authority in your home. The state, through the children, rules this roost. They can remove the children at a whim.

Social workers will be allowed into your home at any time without warning to conduct unsupervised interviews and examinations of your children. They'll have complete authority to remove the child based on subjective determinations of possible abuse or neglect (such as dirty dishes in the sink), or even the perceived "potential" for abuse. However, there is, once again, no clear definition of abuse. You must simply grovel before the social worker's demands. There is one case where a follow-up interview with the child (who was pulled out of his class at school and interviewed without his parents knowledge) resulted in the arrest of the stepfather. The child claimed that the stepfather had "looked at me mean." The police handcuffed the man at his place of work and took him away. Unable to cope with the tyranny of a recalcitrant child, he filed for divorce.

You will probably be required to attend state approved parenting classes, at your own expense. These classes are not likely to advocate the use of spanking, or other emotionally or physically painful disciplines. They focus on the esteem of the child and often feature the "time out" technique. Obviously, this course will attempt to get you to change your values. You will be required to confess your "crime." Undoubtedly, the instructor may be reporting your progress to the court or social services.

You will be forbidden to spank or otherwise discipline your children. These child savers do not believe that a person can control their anger when striking their children. One anti-spanking advocate has been quoted, "After you've hit three or four times, you lose control and just keep whacking!" While this may be true for the speaker, it is patently prejudiced to project their own character weaknesses on everyone else. There are many strong and righteous parents who do not succumb to the animalistic passions that seem to rule so many people in our society today.

Having been denied the ability to effectively enforce your rules, you need to know that the state has absolutely no provisions for controlling disobedient children. I interviewed a social worker who admitted that these children do exert control over the parent's authority in the home and they do recognize it as a problem, however, it is a problem that remains to be resolved. The agents of the state create the problem, then wring their hands and say, "too bad," and leave you to live with it.

If you do spank, they can, and will, take your child

away. But, by this time you may actually be relieved to have the brat he has become out of your hair. Then you will be required to pay for his foster care and face jail time for violating your plea bargain. This is how the system breaks up families.

If your child commits a crime because you have been forbidden to discipline him, you could be held liable for his crime under the burgeoning parent responsibility laws. How can anyone reconcile that with common sense, much less your rights? The state ties your hands regarding controlling your child, and when he gets out of control, punishes you for failing to control him. Does this make sense?

They will often require you to get therapy. They will generally choose the therapist who will be approved by the court. Being approved by the court, his values will likely conflict with yours. He reports to the court regarding your progress. I would seriously question his ethics since your therapy is supposed to be confidential. If you deny the abuse charges, or continue to believe in spanking, he will probably make unsatisfactory reports to the court. Naturally, this will be all on your tab.

The court can also require that your child attend court approved therapy. During these sessions, your child will likely be thoroughly indoctrinated against your repressive and rigid values. You will probably not be informed about anything relating to these sessions. I have knowledge of one of these state sanctioned children's therapists in Western Colorado who has been accused of molesting children on several occasions over several years. The county has knowledge of these allegations, yet he still practices.

Your child's therapist also reports to the court. What does he report? He faithfully reports every private detail about you and your family that your child naively divulges to him. This report is twisted by the social worker before the judge even hears about it.

You will be required to remove all guns from your home. This was one of the terms dictated to us in the plea bargain, even before the gun ban for domestic violence offenders became law. We refused. The child savers claim that violent people tend to use guns against family members and cannot be trusted with guns in the home. They have no evidence to support this claim, but nobody questions it either. This is an attempt at gun control by going through a shady back door. The issue of guns and gun control is completely out of their jurisdiction and a violation of your rights. It is, however, a sterling example of how far they are willing to go to get control over your life.

FAMILY COURT

Most child abuse cases end up in family court. This is a civil court that imposes severe restrictions on the rights of the parents. You will probably be facing some form of a "Dependency and Neglect" (D&N) complaint.

Don't expect to get a jury trial. Family court is an incestuous nest of child savers who view parents as villains totally unworthy of their adorable children. A jury would throw a monkey wrench into their carefully constructed child protection machinery.

In practice, family court judges are rarely impartial. They have aligned themselves with the social workers, and will allow the most outrageous violations of rights to be perpetrated against the parents. If they have not actively aligned themselves with social services, then social services has so much control over what is presented to them that they are totally in the dark regarding the facts of the case. When confronted with these violations, they generally rule against the objection, and proceed to take the word of the social worker as the gospel truth. Social workers stand before judges every day presenting their "evidence" and information without even being put under oath.

Civil court means that the state must prove it's case by a "preponderance of the evidence." This is often explained as the more than 50% rule. If the weight of their evidence equals 51% or more of all the evidence, then the state wins. This isn't too tough to accomplish, especially when the judge routinely disallows the parent's evidence or never sees it, while permitting the state's heresy and perjured evidence. Why? There is a great financial motive for keeping the child under the custody and control of the court.

Many of your witnesses may not be allowed to testify, and much of your taped evidence could be excluded, especially if the judge is corrupt. That doesn't mean you shouldn't gather the evidence and try to get it admitted. You could also create affidavits from the transcripts and file them into the case yourself.

While this may seem like a hopeless endeavor, you do have some tools available to counteract such corruption. Your knowledge of the law will be your biggest asset. You must assert your rights and stand firm. Your ace in the hole is Title 42 U.S.C. sec. 1986, 1985, and 1983.

Most child abuse cases end up in civil court simply because there isn't enough evidence to warrant a criminal trial. As such, there is rarely enough evidence to even allege child abuse. Civil court provides a profitable alternative, and gives the government control over you and the child. That is, if you let them take it.

I'll say it again: I am convinced we didn't have to face the abuses and inequities of family court because we absolutely refused to cooperate with the agents of the state. As a result, they had nothing to use against us. The court has to present at least some appearance of obeying the law, and since social services had nothing to twist and distort, the court could not find any probable cause to start proceedings against us.

Often, if one parent is accused as the abusive parent, the other one will be civilly charged with 'failure to protect.' This is how they get you defending yourself in two courts at once. Even if the charges are dropped against the accused parent, the 'failure to protect' and D&N will be pursued.

CRIMINAL COURT

If you live in a "zero tolerance" jurisdiction, your case will automatically be reviewed for criminal prosecution. While the consequences of conviction are quite dire, including the potential for jail time, you will be greatly relieved to know that common sense is more likely to prevail in criminal court than in family court.

If you demand it, you will get a trial by jury in criminal court. Demand it. Juries are made up of ordinary people, many of whom are parents who believe just the way you do. They have a realistic outlook on parenting and on state intervention of families. Juries are the highest authority in a courtroom, higher than the judge. Juries rarely convict in a child abuse case, especially just for spanking or other reasonable disciplinary measures.

In criminal court, social services must prove their case "beyond a reasonable doubt." This is a much tougher standard than "preponderance of the evidence." "Beyond a reasonable doubt" means they must have overwhelming evidence that you abuse your children, evidence which can leave little or no doubt in the minds of the jury members.

The judge will likely admit more of your valuable

evidence into the record. You will be able to prove that the agents of the state acted unreasonably and aggressively in prosecuting your case. You could even establish evidence of fraudulent, malicious and frivolous proceedings against you and make them responsible for your court costs and attorney fees. I would recommend that you earnestly gather evidence to prove this so you can recover your expenses and make them responsible for their actions.

You will probably have the option of filing an "affirmative defense." The most commonly known affirmative defense is when a person is charged with murder and they claim it was in self-defense. The invocation of "self-defense" is an affirmative defense.

Regarding spanking, Colorado has a statute that addressees the "use of physical force - special relationships.[21]" It states "(1)The use of physical force upon another person which would otherwise constitute an offense is justifiable and not criminal under any of the following circumstances: (a) A parent, guardian, or other person entrusted with the care and supervision of a minor . . . may use reasonable and appropriate physical force upon the minor . . . when and to the extent it is reasonably necessary to maintain discipline or promote the welfare of the minor person . . . " The affirmative defense can completely blow away a prosecutor's case when you demonstrate evidence of appropriate parenting techniques. It requires the prosecutor to establish the guilt of the defendant beyond a reasonable doubt regarding the issue of the affirmative defense as well as to *all* of the elements of the charges filed against him. Many states have similar provisions.

---

[21]C.R.S. 18-1-703

You also have the right to use the Constitution as an affirmative defense. You can challenge the laws that have, piece by piece, stripped parents of their rights to control the upbringing of their children. Only now are parents beginning to raise their voices in protest, albeit weakly and timidly. The agents of the state sense that weakness and go for the jugular. All they have is bluff and intimidation. You must call their bluff.

Unfortunately, a conviction could mean jail time. In our case, we decided to take that risk, because we knew we were right and the state was wrong. It was abusing its authority and power and violating our rights, and we couldn't allow evil to triumph through intimidation. It's not a matter of principle as much as it is a matter of necessity.

You could be risking a false conviction. You can appeal a conviction, and I would strongly recommend it. Statistically, most child abuse convictions are overturned on appeal.

It is time for parents to fight back. If more parents fought the system, it would make it too expensive, and too risky, for the agents of the state to harass law-abiding families. There would be fewer and fewer invasions into the family, and parents could once again, assert control over the family.

But the most important reason to fight is because of the four to five children a day who die at the hands of an abuser. If it became too risky and expensive for social services to attack and prosecute law-abiding parents, they would be forced to concentrate on their only legitimate order of business: Protecting children who are truly abused. There is no sense and no credibility in a system that spends billions of dollars taking custody of children who aren't in danger while it neglects the ones who are being brutally abused. As long as children die and are maimed, those children must be their priority. Social services must be held accountable for their failure to protect the dead and injured.

CHAPTER 8

THE INVESTIGATION

"Just the facts, ma'am." Sergeant Joe Friday, Dragnet

You are under investigation for child abuse. Do you need a lawyer? If you have little or no knowledge of the law, of criminal court procedure, or of the rules of the court, you probably need a lawyer. In fact, most organizations that specialize in false allegations of child abuse insist that you need a lawyer.

But not just any lawyer. You need a lawyer who specializes in false allegations of child abuse and children's law. This is an especially tricky area of the law fraught with deceit and treachery, and your lawyer must know how to fight a winning battle. This area of the law is unlike any other, and a neophyte is guaranteed to earn you a conviction. You don't want to look for the most expensive lawyer, or the most popular lawyer, you want the most experienced lawyer in this area of the law. Anything else will cost you not only money, but your family, and possibly your freedom.

How do you find this lawyer? We found ours through VOCAL, Victims of Child Abuse Laws. This is an organization made up primarily of people who have been falsely accused of one form of child abuse or another. They provide information and a support network to others in the same position. They also offer good, common sense advice. Whether you take it or not is up to you. They, along with other organizations listed in the appendix, can recommend a good lawyer for your case.

Ask your lawyer how much experience he has in dealing with this type of case. Ask how successful he is with these cases, and will he give you references. Satisfy yourself that he is competent to represent you successfully. This is not the time for misplaced loyalties. If you have doubts about your lawyer at any time, get another one that you can trust. There is too much riding on this to trust a mediocre lawyer.

This lawyer will probably be expensive, especially due to the nature of the case. Many lawyers will allow you to make payment arrangements. Many won't. You can also try bartering, especially if you have marketable skills. Offer to do some of your own research, copying or typing to save cost. Don't let the cost of the lawyer prevent you from getting good representation. There's too much at stake. If your lawyer is not amenable to making payment arrangements, perhaps you should find another. This one is obviously more interested in money than principals and he might not be your best advocate in the courtroom.

Having found your lawyer, you must be honest with him. Don't withhold anything pertinent to the case from him. An ugly surprise in the courtroom could cost you your case. You must also make sure he is willing to do what you want him to do. Many lawyers are reluctant to be too aggressive in protecting your rights, especially if they practice law in your community. In truth, as officers of the court, their primary duty is to the court, not to their client. Your lawyer must face this court again, and he doesn't want the judge to hold a grudge against him because of a previous trial. They may not want to present your case as forcefully as you would like it presented.

Since this problem is especially manifest with local lawyers, you might consider hiring a lawyer who practices law in another city, even better, the capital city. This could throw the prosecution and your child's lawyer off guard and tip the scales of justice in your favor. The child's lawyer (often the Guardian Ad Litem) has the unique opportunity to be on the winning side in every case, simply by giving his support to the side that looks like it has an advantage. Why not exploit his vanity and recruit his support for your side by muddying up the waters with an unknown factor; an attorney from out of town? It worked for us.

While you should, to some degree, defer to his judgement, you should also know enough of the law to insist that he protect your interests vigorously. Blind trust in a lawyer, no matter how good he claims to be, is not in your best interest. You'd better familiarize yourself with the statutes in question.

Be prepared to do your own research on the elements relevant to your case, and give your findings to him. You have every right to expect that he will use it in your defense, and you will be helping him to prepare a strong defense for you.

You'll want him to submit every piece of evidence that favors you and object effectively when your rights are violated and when opinion and supposition are presented as fact. Make him understand that this is a battle and the best defense is a strong offense and that failure on his part to take the offensive can open him up to a malpractice lawsuit. If you stay on the defensive, you may as well accept their plea bargain, because you can’t win when they define the battle lines. You must put them on the defensive. Tell your lawyer that you expect him to shred the state's evidence and impeach their witnesses at every opportunity. Make him agree to your terms. If he won't, find another lawyer who will. After all, you are paying for his services and you are entitled to the best he has to give.

This would include many things that are overlooked or dismissed by incompetent lawyers. The first thing a competent attorney should do is hire a private investigator (more on this later in this chapter). If he won’t or doesn’t think it is necessary, ask him if he were charged, would he want one? If not, I'd say, you don't want him to represent you. Don't be afraid to fire an incompetent lawyer, be afraid to have one defend you.

He should tell you to search the child's room for evidence of your child's attitudes, activities, and sexual and social habits. You could find diaries, notes, photos, letters, drawings, phone numbers, drug paraphernalia, videos, books and anything else incriminating. Give copies to your lawyer and investigator.

He should provide you with all court records so you can check them for errors. Many times, simple things like names and dates are wrong. This provides documentation of a pattern of errors made by the agents of the state and can be used to your advantage. You should also check these records for opinions that are presented as facts. Make a list of such things as the social worker's observations regarding the child such as "he was unhappy, indicating he did not want to return home." Did the child say he didn't want to return home, or did the social worker make an unsubstantiated assumption? Keep an eagle eye out for this type of misrepresentation, and make a detailed list for your attorney. He should challenge the validity of every one of the items on your list before the court. Your very freedom and/or the unity of your family depends on the accuracy of these court records, and it is up to you to insure their accuracy. You will also get quite an education on the deceitfulness of the agents of the state.

When social services intervenes in a family, they are required by law to keep records of every interaction. You are allowed by law, to have access to your case file, and to have copies of it. It is illegal for social services to demand that you make your request in writing. Since you are recording all encounters with the agents of the state (including all phone calls), you can verify if they are reporting on these encounters accurately in their case notes, or even if they are recording the encounters at all as required by law. Once again, this will provide valuable evidence of their sloppy and/or biased investigative techniques. If you can prove that they only documented items that could prove detrimental to your case, they will lose an awful lot of credibility before a judge or especially a jury. It could be enough to get the case thrown out.

You are also allowed to have a copy of the social services guidelines, policies and procedures. It could be called by any number of titles, but basically, it is a written manual detailing out the procedures that social workers are *required* to follow during an investigation. This manual should be free, especially if you are involved with social services. When you get this manual, study it with an eye to finding every single time they violated their own guidelines. Make a list of all violations, including dates, and give it to your lawyer. He should use it in court to show how the social worker acted outside her authority when she intervened in your family. It can also be used to sue her personally for civil rights violations against your family.

If you can afford it, hire another attorney. This will stack the deck in your favor. If you watch the coverage of trials involving wealthy people, they always have a team of attorneys. What one attorney missed can be recovered by another. Each parent, stepparent, grandparent, or other close family member could be represented by a different attorney. You want these attorneys to be able to work together toward a common goal, that being the good of the child.

If you are facing criminal charges, and can prove you are indigent, you can have a court appointed attorney. It is highly unlikely a court appointed attorney will represent your best interests. If you're stuck with one, you'll have to work twice as hard to prepare his case for your defense, and really push him into doing what you want him to do. If he refuses, tell the court you are not getting proper representation and you demand another lawyer.

If you are only facing civil charges, you won't be provided with an attorney.

REPRESENTING YOURSELF

Luke 11:46 & 52 And he said, "Woe unto you also, ye lawyers! For ye load men with burdens grievous to be borne, and ye yourselves touch not the burdens with one of your fingers."
"Woe unto you, lawyers! For ye have taken away the key of knowledge: ye entered not in yourselves, and them that were entering in ye hindered." KJV

If you can't afford a lawyer, you might be tempted to represent yourself. There is a growing army of pro se[22] litigants storming the courts these days. The successful ones have spent hundreds of hours learning the law, the rules of procedure, court rulings and any number of other things relating to their case. The advantage of representing yourself is that you can get away with many things a lawyer can't or even won't try. You cannot be held to the same standard of conduct that a lawyer is, the court must make allowances for your inexperience. Because you have everything to lose if you fail, you are inclined to be more daring than a lawyer would be. You are not a lawyer and therefore cannot be censured or disbarred for your daring.

---

[22](Latin) for himself or herself. Pro se representation means that a person will handle his or her own case in court without a lawyer.

Finally, you know your case better than anybody, and can be most effective in presenting it. However, unless you have spent extensive time studying the law and courtroom procedure, and are well prepared to present your case, I would not suggest you represent yourself.

A common mistake pro se defendants make is that they do not argue the law. They'll argue an irrelevant issue like freedom of religion or the constitution. In court, you must address the points of law pertaining to your case. The court isn't interested in anything else.

If you represent yourself, you will have to do everything that was previously described for the lawyer to do. You will be responsible for getting all the records and information in your own defense. Learn about discovery and push to get all the records related to your case.

There are law study groups all over the country, and there are many books written on how to represent yourself in court. Sometimes, the information is very contradictory from one group or book to the next. If you are going to attempt your own defense, it might not be a bad idea to hook up with one of these groups for guidance and support. I can assure you, lawyers hold such groups in pretty high disdain, probably because many of the groups advocate tactics and points of law that a lawyer wouldn't or couldn't touch.

Many law study groups such as the American De Jure Alliance and Right Way l.a.w. rely on points of law that are represented by constitutional and common law principles which are not applicable to corporations. Lawyers only practice law as it applies to corporations. Members will insist on not being designated as pro se or pro per (in the proper person) before the court because that means they are acting as a lawyer, giving representation to themselves, and that invalidates their status as a living, natural born person. They've discovered that only corporations require the representation of a lawyer in court. Living people are not corporations and are therefore entitled to the protections of the constitution that are not available to any other legal entity. This is very complicated to learn but very simple to apply effectively because it is based on one legal concept: Fraud. Although it is very unorthodox, I've seen it work. It's complicated enough for a book in and of itself so I can't go into detail here. If you are interested, look for Right Way l.a.w. in the appendix.

POLICE INVESTIGATION

In a criminal proceeding, the police are going to want to question you, and maybe even your children, in order to obtain evidence against you. It is simple enough for you to refuse to answer any of their questions or to refuse them access to your children. However, if they subpoena your children, you cannot prevent this questioning. You and/or your lawyer will have to ask the court to set specific conditions for this interrogation and to limit it to one session to avoid traumatizing the child. This will be a hard-ball tactic. If you do it properly, the court will have to comply or face a lawsuit for violating your rights.

In order to insure that the information obtained is not biased or tainted, insist that your lawyer and/or pastor and/or family therapist is present at the questioning. Your representative must be informed and knowledgeable of the suggestive techniques often used to lead a child to say what the agents of the state want to hear. They must recognize this technique when it is used on your children and object to it each time it happens. Their job is to insure that the child is not asked leading questions or emotionally traumatized by the process. This session must be videotaped to preserve the evidence for the trial.

If the judge refuses your request, I would not accept his order as final. I would appear with my child at the appointed time and place and refuse to let the child out of my arms or out of my sight. If I could get the press to accompany me, I'd do it. I'd have my trusted advocates, and as many supporters as I could muster, accompany me with their video cameras rolling. I would not refuse to let them question my child, thereby honoring the subpoena, but I would insist that I be present at the questioning to protect him, because he is minor and as his parent, I have that right. I would make them forcibly remove my child from my arms *on camera* to prove how far they are willing to go to violate my rights, then publicize it as widely as I could. Your lawyer will undoubtedly advise against it, but lawyers aren't fond of dramatic tactics. Neither is the court, they don't like that kind of publicity one bit. They may even back off and honor your original request, which is what you want. If not, I'd present my Title 42 paperwork with the judge's, the prosecutor's, the social worker's, and anyone else involved, names already typed on, to them and march right down to the Federal court and file my lawsuit against them.

If your child is subpoenaed, you can teach him to say only one thing in answer to any question, "According the Privacy Act of 1974, I don't have to answer any question without my parents being present." If he says this before his is taken into seclusion, while the tapes are rolling and the witnesses are present, you will have plenty of evidence for your lawsuit if they still take the child and question him outside of your presence. They cannot, by law, question him after he has invoked the Privacy Act, whether he has invoked in your presence or not. Since the state receives federal money, they are bound by law to observe the Privacy Act of 1974.

To impeach the testimony that the child might give

under the state's influence, you'll want to have your own expert witness, a psychologist or therapist, speak with the child after this interview. This expert can bring to light information about how the child felt during the state's interrogation, including if the child was scared or pressured into saying something that wasn't true. He can also use the child's testimony to verify that there was no abuse inflicted on the child. This should also be videotaped.

If there is no subpoena issued, do not allow your child to be questioned or examined by the agents of the state.

Do not sign any paperwork. I repeat, DO NOT SIGN ANY PAPERWORK. If they make you sign, saying you'll go to jail or you'll lose your children if you don't sign, include a statement above your signature, "Signed under threat, duress, and coercion." This statement will automatically invalidate your signature because you did not sign of your own free will. Be sure to make them threaten you with something if you do not sign before using this statement. Do not agree to any terms. Do not talk to anyone. If you tell them you don't want to talk, they must honor that.

SOCIAL SERVICES INVESTIGATION

The social worker will continue to contact you to come in for an appointment. She'll show up at your door. She wants to talk to you and your children. Don't do it. Demand that she stop harassing you without cause or you will file a complaint. Be aware that she may try to get others to file false complaints against you. If there is suddenly a rash of complaints against you that must be investigated, suspect your social worker. Hire a private investigator, or conduct your own investigation to expose this abuse of process and fraud, then press charges. She can be put in jail. At the very least, you will be assigned a different case worker. You can also press charges against those who conspired with her to make false accusations against you, and I would demand they face trial for their actions.

She may offer you some paperwork to sign, often a form that states you requested the intervention of social services to assist your family. Don't sign it. She may tell you it means nothing. It's only a formality. She's lying. Don't sign it. If you do, you'll have given written permission for them to invade your home and stick to your family like leeches, and it will be used against you in court.

She'll threaten you with jail, except she won't tell you she doesn't have the authority to put you in jail. She'll threaten to bring the police. Don't give in. If she does bring the police, ask for the warrant. If they don't have it, ask them to leave. If they claim your child is in imminent danger, prove them wrong, then ask them to leave. Your home is inviolate, and only you can make them honor that. They can only come in if you invite them or let them. Otherwise they are breaking the law and you can nail them for it.

YOUR OWN INVESTIGATION

You'll also want to immediately hire your own private investigator. He will conduct an investigation of you and your family, to verify that you have no history of violent behavior, criminal activity, drug use, etc. You should also have him find out how many other families have been unjustly harassed by this social worker, investigator, and anyone else involved in your "persecution." This includes doctors who reported that your child was abused. How many complaints and/or lawsuits have been lodged against these people? What was the outcome of these complaints/lawsuits? You'll also want him to verify the backgrounds of all the people involved, including their education and training, and their status in their respective classes (e.g., did they barely pass, are they losers?). Have him look specifically for evidence that they might have felt themselves to be abused as children and whether they might have an irrational tendency to react hysterically to allegations of child abuse. Find out if other parents have been abused by their intervention. He'll also need to dig up evidence of substance abuse. Your goal is to destroy their personal and professional credentials and credibility. This is another thing that your lawyer may be reluctant to do, but it is in your best interest. After all, they have tried to destroy your personal and parental credentials and credibility.

Your defense investigation must also include the gathering of evidence in your favor such as your child's journal or notes which might prove there was no abuse. Information gathered from your child's friends could prove invaluable. Your witnesses will also provide evidence in your defense.

You will want to investigate possible motives of the child in making the allegation, and of the person who reported the allegation. This should include complete background checks.

You will need an expert in psychological motives, who can recognize various psychological reasons for certain behaviors, and recognize programming of the child. A child can be programmed by rehearsing or coaching the child regarding his testimony. This type of coaching is often done by therapists, counselors, social workers, and prosecutors. Your investigator will want to discover how many times this rehearsing is conducted. Additionally, programming occurs when a child gets positive reinforcement for his allegations and negative reinforcement for denying the allegations, and when the child is effectively isolated from anyone who questions the truth of the accusation.

You will need to discover if the investigation has been contaminated, for example, the child didn't get the elements supporting his accusation from the alleged incident, but rather from outside sources. Your investigator will need to find the sources of contamination. When my Jacob began to "own" the abusive experiences of the other children in treatment with him, this was a form of contamination.

Many times, the child wants to appear in court, especially if he has recanted a false allegation, but social services won't permit him to present his story to the judge. I would suggest that you or your lawyer subpoena the child as a witness. This is one method whereby social services can be compelled to allow the child into the courtroom. Another method, have the child write out his story, sign it and file it into the court record. Let him use his own words, don't coach him at all.

I can't say it enough . . . Don't let anyone into your home without a warrant . . . Don't answer any questions . . . Don't sign anything . . . Don't let them question or examine your children.

PUBLICITY

I have already made references to getting the press involved in your fight. This is a hard tactic to accomplish, since the media is often afraid to get involved in such a subjective issue. However, happily, this mood is changing with regard to family intervention. You should have your trusted advocates and friends write letters to the editor. If the paper gets enough of these letters, a few of them are bound to get published. It could even spark an investigation of their own. Call the television and radio stations asking for coverage of court events or of your story.

Write to your representatives. All of them, local, state and federal. Have your family members write to theirs. Tell them your story in two pages or less, and make an emotional pitch like, "Social services is trying to force us to lie to get our children back." Hit them below the belt with the truth. This is how laws get changed, and the more letters, the faster the laws change. Copy (cc:) these letters to as many people as possible, including heads of organizations, broadcasters and influential community leaders.

See about putting your videotapes of the agents of the state abusing your family's rights on local cable access channels. There are many programs out there that address all areas of government abuses and this would provide great programming for them, as well as to publicize your problem.

Start a legal defense fund to pay for your legal fees, and include that information with every outlet that you release your story to. This will only work if you publicize your story widely.

Broadcast it on the Internet. Set up a home page and contact the news groups.

Call talk radio shows with your story and tapes. Arrange to be a guest and let the world know about the evil child protection system. Send letters to the hosts for them to read on the air.

See if you can get the local news teams interested in your story, especially if another local child has recently died at the hands of an abusive family member. They can present an excellent news story as to why are children who aren't in danger taken from their parents while truly abused children are murdered instead of being protected by social services.

Social services is in bad public favor these days. They've screwed up too often and cost the lives of innocent children while they conducted frantic witch hunts against decent families. These decent families have taken to the airwaves and the street with their cries of protest. The agents of the state HATE publicity. Publicity shines the light of truth on their dark and dirty secrets. They often put up a defiant front but if you push it hard enough, and back your claims with your mountains of evidence, they could end up dropping you like a hot potato.

CHAPTER 9

THE TRIAL

"In a child abuse case, you are guilty until proven innocent." A Universal Truth.

PRETRIAL

You're going to trial. Whether it is a civil or criminal trial, the procedures are basically the same. Your lawyer will handle most of the pre-trial preparations. There will probably be a pre-trial conference with the prosecutor. There is the process of discovery where each side is entitled to the information that the other side has related to the case. There will be motions and possibly motions hearings, to determine what will be excluded from the trial and numerous other legal issues.

Your lawyer should take an aggressive posture, and ask for everything he can think of. He should bury the prosecution in paperwork while vigorously demanding protection of your rights and challenging the smallest violation thereof. This will accomplish two things: it will make the prosecution's case much more expensive than they anticipated, and it will provide valuable groundwork for your case and for an appeal if necessary.

Social services and the other agents of the state will not be willing to give up records that might prove beneficial to your case, even they are required to by law. You'll have to fight diligently for every shred of information during discovery.

Be sure to also get school records and police reports which very often contradict social services records and can provide valuable evidence to impeach state witnesses. You'll also want to have the social services' policies and procedures, all paperwork filed with the state and/or federal governments, and the complete case files related to your case. Close examination will reveal that they didn't even follow their own agency requirements during the investigation. Anyone who has had contact with your children, pastor, doctor, etc. should have some kinds of records regarding your children. Get them.

APPEARANCES COUNT

When you appear before a judge, it is important that you make the proper impression. You want to appear upright and respectable. You should dress as though you were going to church. Men, wear a conservative suit and tie; women, a modest suit or dress and hose. Polish your shoes. Your hair should be clean and well groomed in a conservative style. Do not wear garish jewelry or excessive makeup.

Your supporters should also be neatly groomed and well behaved. That means no outbursts or noise during the trial.

You must get to the courthouse on time.

Your defense must be based on the law, not Biblical precepts or constitutional rights. Do not attempt to interject your personal beliefs during the trial. Stick to the issue at hand, that being the law.

If you are having a jury trial, the first step will be the selection of the jury. This will be achieved by the process of "voir dire" (vwah deer). Each lawyer will be able to ask questions of each potential juror. These questions are designed to reveal the attitudes of the juror and are used to eliminate jurors who might be predisposed for or against one side or the other. Each side has an equal number of times that they can excuse a juror without giving a reason, known as peremptory challenge. Once that number is used up, you're stuck with what's left.

Dismissing a juror for cause is requested by one of

the lawyers and granted or denied by the judge. Cause includes reasons such as: The juror personally knows one of the parties to the case, or the juror has been personally involved in this type of a case before, or the juror is obviously biased on this issue.

The number of jurors will depend on the rules in your jurisdiction. It can take several hours or even longer to select a jury. You will notice that the lawyers are very respectful to the jurors as they question them. They also make it a point to remember each juror's name and to address them personally. There's no sense in antagonizing them. They will be making the decision in this case.

Of course, you will be observing all this. Perhaps your lawyer will consult with you regarding certain jurors, or you may want to have him ask a specific question. Your lawyer shouldn't leave you out of this process. Your insight could be helpful.

Once the jury has been selected, the trial can begin. First there will be the opening arguments. With the prosecution going first, each side will present an overview of the case they will present. They will be speaking directly to the jury. The prosecution is going to try and make you look like a child beater, or an uncaring parent, or anything else they can think of. You'd better be prepared for it, and don't let it get you angry. It's very difficult to sit there quietly and let someone lie about you, but you've got to maintain your composure.

After the opening arguments are complete, the prosecution will present its case. There are very specific rules regarding the testimony of witnesses and the introduction of evidence. If these rules are not followed, the testimony or the evidence can be disallowed. For example, witnesses have to establish their credibility before they are allowed to testify, verifying they actually witnessed the event. An expert witness must establish their credentials with the court, proving their expertise in a specific subject. A witness must also usually validate a piece of evidence before it can be admitted into evidence. This is why the lawyer will ask a witness to identify an item and verify it's authenticity as they introduce it to the court. They will also let the jurors examine it at that time.

If a witness or item of evidence has not been properly validated, one of the lawyers will likely object. If the objection is sustained, the other lawyer must provide further validation or drop the ploy he was attempting. If the objection is denied, the objecting lawyer must provide proof, such as case law or statute, to support his objection, or let the other lawyer continue.

Lawyers are not permitted to ask “leading questions” of witnesses. These are questions that would give the witness a clue to the answer that the lawyer was looking for. All questions must be phrased to elicit the facts from the witness without putting ideas or words into their heads. Leading questions should be objected to and sustained.

Witnesses are notified about the trial in advance. Any witness unwilling to testify can be subpoenaed by either side and compelled to testify. This is the actual function of a legal subpoena. Both sides have the right to subpoena witnesses who don't want to testify. These people will be treated as hostile witnesses.

A hostile witness may not be forthcoming with his testimony, and the court will allow leading questions to be used to extract the testimony from them.

If a lawyer asks the witness a question that has nothing to do with the issues before the court, the other lawyer will object saying it is irrelevant. The Judge will then rule on the relevance of the question.

Witnesses are not allowed in the courtroom during the trial. This is so they not hear what other witnesses say, which might contaminate their own testimony, and they are not allowed to talk to other witnesses. This is to be sure that they do not compare stories or change their stories.

As the prosecution calls its witnesses and builds its case, you will be shocked to find out how many agents of the state lie under oath. This is common practice, and there is little you can do about it. Hopefully, their testimony will be discounted by the jury as being without credibility. It is unlikely they will ever be charged with perjury.

The presentation by the prosecution is certain to anger you. It is designed to be offensive to you and to get you to react emotionally. It will likely be untrue. You must not react. Remain calm.

Another nasty item is that in some states, your spouse may be compelled to be a witness for the prosecution. That means to be a witness against you. In Colorado, the incident of privileged communication between husband and wife shall not be a ground for excluding evidence in any judicial proceeding[23] involving a child abuse case. This has been known to backfire in the prosecution's face, especially when the parents are not abusive.

Your children may also testify.

The people who interviewed your child will be allowed to testify about what the child said to them. This is known as hearsay. Hearsay is disallowed in any trial except a child abuse trial. This is one of the ways the system is rigged against parents. In our trial, this hearsay evidence was given by a school counselor. Then the police investigator got up and testified about what the

---

[23]C.R.S. 13-3-111(2)

counselor had told him that Jacob had told her. Second and even third hand hearsay is admissible in a child abuse trial!

I'm sure you've played the game of "telephone," where everyone sits in a circle and the first person whispers a message to the next person in line. This message is passed around the circle and the last person repeats it out loud. The massage has been drastically changed and in no way even resembles the original message. This is great for laughs as a game, but it can be devastating when a person's family and freedom are at stake. It is patently immoral to allow hearsay testimony in any court of law.

After the prosecution is finished with each witness, your lawyer will have the opportunity to cross-examine the witness. He must limit himself to the issues that were brought up by the prosecuting attorney's questioning. Your lawyer will attempt to impeach each witness or their testimony. This means he will show that the witness is untruthful, either by evidence of past conduct or by showing directly that the witness is not telling the truth. This is where the evidence gathered by your private investigator is valuable.

Your lawyer will also take the opportunity to have the witness clarify or elaborate on any points that are in your favor. Finally, make sure your lawyer asks the questions you think are important, even if he doesn't think they are. I have been involved in several trials, and each time I asked my lawyer to bring up a specific point, he declined saying it wasn't necessary. After the trial, members of the jury confirmed my instincts were correct. If the lawyer had presented the information I requested, it would have affected the jury's decision more in my favor. Trust your instincts and make your lawyer comply with your wishes.

After the cross examination, the prosecution can ask more questions, but he must still stick to the issues already brought up in the cross-examination. This is called redirect. Finally the defense will re-cross, sticking to the issues brought up in the redirect. Having presented all its witnesses and evidence, the prosecution concludes it's case.

At this time your lawyer may request a directed verdict. This motion may be written or verbal. He is asking the Judge to rule on whether or not the prosecution has presented enough evidence for a rational person to conclude that you committed a crime. It is unlikely that the Judge will grant the motion, but it should be part of the record if the prosecution's case didn't establish that you committed a crime. And they often don't.

Now will be your lawyer's turn to present your defense. The procedure will be identical to the prosecution's presentation. This is where you get to present your evidence, including all the tapes you have which record the actions by the agents of the state. The prosecutor will try to keep these out of evidence. Failing that, he will try to discredit this evidence. If the Judge disallows this evidence, and you get convicted, you will have grounds to have the conviction overturned on appeal. A court cannot deny relevant evidence that could prove beneficial for your case without violating your rights.

Your lawyer will question your witnesses. You will want to have your own expert witnesses to contradict what the prosecution's expert witnesses testified to.

You'll want your own expert witness to testify to psychological reasons for the child's accusation. There are many psychological syndromes that can cause a false accusation, such as Parental Alienation Syndrome, and here is where you have the opportunity to prove it.

You will also want an expert medical witness to

testify about the absence of injury, or to explain what might cause the injury in question. This can be accompanied by scientific studies to validate the expert opinion. There is an example of a case where a child suffered a spiral fracture in the leg as his father changed the child's diaper. This father routinely lifted only one of the child's legs to slip the diaper under this baby's bottom. A worldwide search of scientific studies proved the father did not abuse the child, but provided substantial evidence as to the cause of the fracture, and demonstrated the small amount of repeated force needed to cause such a fracture. You never know what you will find that can be valuable in your own defense, unless you look. Once you find the appropriate studies, you must also find a witness who is expert in this area of knowledge to present it to the court.

Expert witnesses usually charge an "expert witness" fee for appearing in court. This is hardly something to quibble about with so much at stake. Find a way to work it out financially. It could mean the difference between acquittal and conviction.

TAKING THE STAND

One big decision you and your lawyer will have to make is whether or not you will take the stand in your own defense.

You are not required to do so. While a jury is not supposed to hold it against you if you do not take the stand in your own defense, human nature dictates that they just might think you have something to hide.

The problem with taking the stand is that the prosecution will have two chances to question you, the cross-examination and the re-cross. He's eager for you to take the stand, especially if you have refused to answer questions during the investigation. He thinks he can nail you. You have to be very careful not to say anything that could damage your case. The prosecutor will twist your words and answers into something you didn't mean.

Here's an example of how they will manipulate you emotionally:

My husband, Dennis, took the stand in his own defense. After his lawyer finished questioning him, the prosecutor cross-examined him. She tried very hard to goad him into anger. She used words like "beat" and "whip." She made nasty remarks about his great size and power (he's 6'2" with broad shoulders and strong arms) in comparison to little tiny Jacob (she had never seen Jacob) who was as tall as I at the time. I figured that made him adult sized, and it also made him taller than the prosecutor. Go figure. She didn't make him angry. She made herself look foolish. Dennis was able to credibly dispute all her outrageous allegations of his brutality.

Then she picked up the martinet. She tried to get him to admit it was an instrument of torture, but he didn't. He calmly explained how it was designed not to cause injury without being apologetic for having decided to use it. He admitted that the purpose of using it was to cause some pain, that's what a spanking is for, whether the child savers like it or not. Then she pulled out what she thought was her ace in the hole; she demanded that he duplicate the spanking for the jury. She instructed him to strike himself on the leg with the martinet with the same force and number of swats he used on Jacob's bottom. I could see the anger in his eyes, a truly frightening look to anyone who is ignorant of his righteous character. He paused and drew the leather strands through his hand, then proceeded to strike himself in the leg eight times with the martinet. It was essentially the same spanking he had give Jacob. His face was grim, but he controlled his emotions. Having completed this demonstration, he calmly held the martinet out to the prosecutor for her to take it. The anger was gone from his eyes. She took it without a word. What could she say? His gaze returned to the jury, open and forthright.

Dennis had effectively blown the prosecutor's case. He had demonstrated that he could and would control his emotions no matter how provoked he was and could administer a spanking dispassionately without using excessive force. And the child savers say it can't be done.

How you behave on the stand is very important. You must not appear to be giving evasive answers. Address your answers directly to the jury, even though the lawyer is addressing the questions to you. Make eye contact with the jury members while you answer.

If you are unsure of a question, it is all right to say you don't understand and make the lawyer rephrase it. If the lawyer asks you long, complicated questions, don't answer them. You could become confused and give a wrong answer. Ask him politely to make it simpler to understand. Make him repeat the question in such a manner that your answer cannot be perverted into something that you didn't mean. Give short concise answers; Yes and No are the best kind of answer. When you give longer answers, be precise in the use of your words. You can also make the prosecutor be precise by asking him to define what he means by using such a word.

For example, in Dennis' case, he was asked if he beat Jacob. He replied with a simple 'no'. If he had been pressed by the prosecutor, he could have asked "What exactly is the definition of 'beat'?" This would have guaranteed that everybody was communicating on the same wavelength. The prosecutor cannot define a "beating" the same as a spanking, the jury wouldn't buy it and he'd lose credibility.

You must answer all questions asked unless your lawyer objects and the judge sustains the objection. You can also refuse to answer if you don't want to be a witness against yourself, but it looks bad to the jury when you do that. See first if your lawyer will object to the question as irrelevant or vague. You can always say you don't understand the question and make him rephrase it. However, do not answer any more than just what the lawyer asks; do not volunteer anything. If an important point must be brought out, your lawyer will ask you the appropriate questions to bring it out. If you are unsure about answering a question put to you by the prosecution, look at your lawyer for help, he may be ready to object.

Pause slightly before answering each question to allow your lawyer an opportunity to object if he needs to. Address the lawyer who is asking the questions as sir or ma'am, even if you despise him. Finally, try not to get too emotional on the stand. Maintain your composure and save the emotions for outside the courtroom.

If you are reading this book, you are probably an aware parent. Aware of the dangers that lurk outside your door when it comes to disciplining your children. As such, you are protecting yourself and your family regarding your discipline actions. The prosecutor will construe this to mean that you acting deliberately and with premeditation, and trying to hide your "crime." It came up when I was on the stand, and it just might when you are, too.

They'll want to know if and why you examined the child's bottom for bruising after a spanking. Just state the truth, that you know there are people out there who want to take your children away on the slightest pretext and that you just wanted to establish for the record that you are not abusive just in case someone tried to falsely accuse you of being abusive. You also wanted to be able to verify there was no injury to the child just in case someone would falsely claim there was injury. It's not unlike buying insurance for your house or wearing a seat belt in your car. Does buying insurance mean you intend to burn your house down? Does wearing a seat belt mean you intend to have an accident? Of course not. They are means by which you protect yourself from damage caused by events beyond your control. This is no different.

The other tactics described in this book will also be construed against you: recording the spanking sessions, the affidavits you collected in your defense, if you prepared a prearranged safe house for your children in the event social services tried to put them in a foster home, and your recordings of all dealings with agents of the state. Simply say you had reason to believe you were being targeted for false allegations of child abuse and you wanted to have evidence in your defense. If the prosecutor says something about that being rather paranoid, you can say something like, "Well, here I am in just that situation. Is that paranoia or preparation?"

It is imperative that, as a witness, you are sincere and project credibility. Much can be read into your body language and your genuinely earnest responses to the questions asked.

The defendant will probably be the final witness for the defense.

After the defense has concluded, the prosecution can call rebuttal witnesses to rebut the testimony of the defense witnesses. Then the defense can present your rebuttal witnesses to rebut the prosecution's rebuttal witnesses.

The last actions will be the closing statements. With the prosecution going first, each side will sum up the case, reminding the jury of all the points of law, testimony, and evidence that support their case. The defense will follow, and the prosecution will have the last word, because they (supposedly) have the burden of proof.

The judge will then give instructions to the jury

regarding the law and their duty. These instructions have been prepared by the lawyers and the Judge decides which ones he will allow the jury to hear. Some of your instructions could be denied by the Judge.

The jurors then leave the courtroom to deliberate in private. They will have all the evidence with them to help them consider the case. They may also ask the court for transcripts or clarification on points they are unclear about.

It is impossible to tell what moves a jury, so trying to guess what the outcome will be is an exercise in futility. It's an anxiety-ridden time waiting for the verdict. Try to be as calm as possible.

When the jury has reported that it has reached a verdict, you will be ordered to return to the courtroom. Your emotions will be in turmoil as you await the reading of the verdict. There will probably be law enforcement officers standing near you to take you away in the event that the verdict is guilty. Try to ignore them. They're just doing their job.

You may be asked to stand as the verdict is read. If it is not guilty, you're free to go. Social services is most likely out of your life, and you can more effectively keep them out, now. You can now try to repair the damage to your family that they caused.

If it comes back guilty, you might be handcuffed immediately and taken away. Don't fight it.

The judge might also set an appeal bond. This will allow you to remain out of jail during your appeal. And you should appeal. Remember, the majority of child abuse convictions are overturned on appeal. All the evidence that the judge denied in this trial will be used as part of your grounds to have the conviction overturned, as high as 90%! You can also appeal on the basis of "ineffective assistance of counsel" if your lawyer didn't represent your case effectively. In order to pull this one off, you'll probably have to sue him for malpractice.

CHAPTER 10

JURY DUTY

"The jury has the right to judge both the law as well as the fact in controversy." John Jay, 1st Chief Justice US supreme court, 1789

"The law itself is on trial quite as much as the cause which is to be decided." Harlan F. Stone, 12th Chief Justice, US supreme court, 1941

"The pages of history shine on instances of the jury's exercise of its prerogative to disregard instructions of the judge . . ." U.S. vs. Dougherty, 473 F 2nd 1113, 1139, (1972)

Today's juries are manned by ignorant Americans who have no knowledge of the power of the jury or of the obscene injustices perpetrated by a court that is not constrained by a fully informed jury. This is due in part to the overwhelming attitude that jury duty is an intrusion into your profits and time, and due in part to the conspiracy of the bench that abhors a fully informed juror and endeavors to oust any potential juror who displays the smallest glimmer of knowledge regarding the real role of the jury.

Because the average American cannot bear to perform his civic duty on the jury lest he misses work, we largely get the bottom of the barrel of our society to serve as jurors. These are often the TV talk show junkies and recipients of the government handout, the lowest common denominator of our society. They follow orders well and don't have an independent thought in their heads. They couldn't tell you what the Bill of Rights was, or participate in a logical debate on corruption in the government.

That isn't to say there aren't good jurors out there, but they are badly outnumbered.

What is a good juror? A good juror is honest and impartial. He can listen well and pick up subtle nuances in testimony. But most of all, he knows how the judicial system is supposed to operate as opposed to how it actually does operate. He knows the abuses of the system, and can recognize a bad law, a bad prosecutor, a bad defendant, a bad lawyer for the defense, a bad cop, and a bad judge. He knows that the jury is the highest authority in the courtroom and he is willing to exercise that authority.

Where the courts consistently side with the other agents of the government, the juror is impartial.

Where the prosecutor is more interested in winning the case than in discovering the truth, the juror seeks the truth.

Where the law violates the rights of Americans, the juror will nullify that law with his verdict.

Where the judge instructs unconstitutionally, the juror ignores the instructions and votes on the verdict constitutionally.

Where he may be battered and abused by other jurors who are ignorant or biased and who want him to compromise his vote, he will stand firm on his principals and the constitution. It only takes one fully informed juror to educate the rest of the jury, or failing that, to cause a mistrial.

The courts are not going to tell you, the jury, that you are the highest authority, because then they couldn't keep doing what they've been doing. The prosecutor has the most to lose if you are fully informed, because he depends on jury ignorance to violate the rights of the accused with impunity. The prosecutor and the judge will block all instructions and other information from the jury that might inform them of their actual authority. It is up to you to be knowledgeable before you step into that jury box.

As a juror, you are not compelled to follow the judge's instructions to the jury. You are not even compelled to follow the law as it is presented to you by the court. Your highest obligation is to the constitution and to justice. These are concepts that are rarely found in today's courtrooms.

That isn't to say that there aren't righteous judges out there. In fact, I believe that we had a fairly decent judge for my husband's trial. She seemed to be fair and was genuinely concerned about the law. Maybe it was because she was one of the rare judges that wasn't a lawyer.

The concept of jury nullification predates the Declaration of Independence. William Penn's life was spared in 1670 because four jurors refused to join eight others and convict him for preaching a different view of the Bible than that of the Church of England; a capital offense. These four jurors refused to bow to the demands of the court and endured nine weeks of torture in prison. They knew that the law that brought Penn into court was a bad law, and by their "not guilty" votes, the "Conventicle Act" was struck down.

The jury gives the people the power to stem the tide of oppression and tyranny that is caused by the creation of bad laws. These are laws that are created to punish those who have not committed any act which causes injury to someone's person or property, which is the true definition of a crime. Jury nullification is a powerful tool to invalidate unconstitutional and unrighteous laws. It is not only a juror's right, but his duty to nullify bad laws with his not guilty vote.

Besides protecting the person charged with nonexistent crimes, jury nullification protects your rights as well. The fewer viable bad laws there are, the more freedoms we all will enjoy.

When you get called for jury duty, it is in your personal best interest to serve. You have power over the judge, the congress and the President to nullify bad laws and to protect the rights of Americans. You can also protect them by convicting true criminals which validates the good laws.

If you sit on a child abuse case, you must determine if the law is righteous *as well as* if the accused is guilty. If it is true child abuse, which could also be assault and/or battery, then you must convict. If not, send the strongest possible message to the court that these abusive actions against innocent citizens cannot be tolerated. Nullify the law with your not guilty vote, and don't let yourself be swayed by ignorant or weak-willed jurors.

It is especially important to vote your conscience without being intimidated into compromising your vote because the Supreme Court has recently ruled that even though a person may not be convicted by a jury of all the crimes he was charged with, the judge is permitted to consider all the crimes he was charged with when sentencing him for the ones he was convicted of.

Prosecutors routinely stack as many charges as possible on a defendant based on the "manure principle": That if you throw enough manure at the side of a barn, some of it is bound to stick. They know most juries will feel that if a person has so many charges against him, he must have done something wrong and so they feel they must find the defendant guilty of something, even if it's only the jaywalking charge.

Now the Supreme Court has made it possible for judges to sentence a defendant as if he were convicted of all the charges, not just the jaywalking charge. Juries can no longer operate on the "manure principle." As a juror, you need to know the psychological concept behind stacking charges against a defendant, and not allow yourself to be manipulated into finding an innocent man or woman guilty just to satisfy the "manure principle." It has never been more critical to practice jury nullification to stem the tide of tyranny.

THE GRAND JURY

There is another kind of jury duty you might be called for: The Grand Jury. This is not a one day or one trial service. Grand jurors serve for a specified amount of time. This is the body of people who hand down the indictments which bring people to trial.

Court yourself truly fortunate if you are called to serve on a grand jury. You will have enormous power and authority to clean up the corrupt judicial system, but only if you know how to use it.

Historically, prosecutors where never allowed into the grand jury room. Today, they are calling all the shots, and even ordering grand jurors around. Ignorant of the true role of the grand jury, these jurors meekly comply. The grand jury process today has been perverted by the practice of allowing the prosecution to run the proceedings. As proof of this, there is a common saying that a prosecutor could get a grand jury to "indict a ham sandwich." Is this justice?

Author and talk radio show host, Mike Brown, has an excellent tape set on the history and power of the grand jury. If you get called, I'd recommend you get those tapes. He is listed in the appendix.

If I were chosen to serve on a grand jury, the first

thing I would do is to teach the other grand jurors of the constitutional role of the grand jury simply by playing Mike Brown's two tapes to the other jurors during our first session together, or by giving them copies of the tapes to take home. Then we'd severely limit or eliminate the prosecutor's participation in the proceedings. Grand jurors should call the witnesses, not the prosecutor. If the prosecutor fails to make his case, I'd issue a no bill (this means I would not indict) and not allow him to make numerous additional appearances to present additional bits and pieces of evidence until he gets his indictment. He'd have to have his ducks in a row the first time, or lose his case for all time. If he tried to act outside his authority and charge any of the grand jury members, I'd put *him* under investigation. The prosecution, as an agent of the state, has had entirely too much control over our country's grand juries to the detriment of our freedom.

Our jury system was designed to act as both a sword and a shield. It is supposed to protect the people against government abuses of power and to prosecute and punish criminals. Today, violent criminals are protected while righteous Americans are prosecuted. The only way to reverse this trend is for righteous and knowledgeable people to serve on as many juries as possible. Nullify the bad laws and refuse to indict innocent people. This is very likely our last line of defense against tyranny.

CHAPTER 11

ACCOUNTABILITY AND DAMAGES

*"All of the law and case law is against them, so they've created this line of bulls**t." Peter Jon Simpson, publisher of the* Irwin Rommel School of Law.

You've heard the horror stories about families destroyed because of irrational witch hunts spearheaded by Social Services. We've anguished over the tragedies of children removed from their loving parents; children who are then coerced and deceived into making false allegations of abuse against their parents by the agents of the state. Of families bankrupted and parents jailed based on lies and innuendo, of parental rights terminated without genuine due process in legally sanctioned kangaroo style family courts.

You've been told smugly by the lawyers and agents of the state that you have no recourse. There's that impenetrable "immunity clause" which protects the actions of the amoral child savers, allowing them to act maliciously against righteous parents without restraint or consequence. Is it true, in America, that after someone has stolen all that was important to you that you cannot even hope for your day in court to recover your damages?

That's what they'd like you to think. But you must remember, the agents of the state are accomplished liars. Nothing else they've ever said during the entire child abuse investigation has been true, so why should this be any different? It's a lie. You do have recourse in the form of a powerful tool. This tool is 42 U.S.C. (United States Code) sections 1986, 1985 and 1983.

42 U.S.C. sec. 1986 deals with "having knowledge of the law and did or witness wrongs and neglected to

correct and prevent" those wrongs. 42 U.S.C. sec. 1985 deals with "conspiracy to interfere with civil rights." Paragraph (3) addresses "depriving persons of rights or privileges," and allows for the recovery of damages due to their actions that deprived you of your rights and applies to individuals who cause you injury by depriving you of your rights. 42 U.S.C. sec. 1983 permits "Civil action for deprivation of rights." This section specifically applies to state officials acting under the color of state laws, and violating your rights in the process.

If we examine this closely, I'm sure you can think of numerous rights that were violated during the investigation, by people who, in all likelihood, knew they were violating your rights. You probably even informed them they were violating your rights and can establish they had knowledge and neglected to correct or prevent those violations. How about your right to due process, your fundamental liberty and privacy interest in maintaining the integrity of your family unit, your right against illegal searches and seizures, your right to equal protection of the law, your freedom of association and religion, or any other various and sundry rights that are casually trampled during a child abuse witch hunt? Add to that other offenses like kidnaping and false imprisonment (including your children who were placed in foster care), assault and battery and/or sexual molestation (unasked for medical exams of your children), loss of consortium, intentional and/or negligent infliction of mental distress, willful interference with family relations, etc. Investigation of the statutes will reveal how you and your family were injured.

One important key is to hit them hard and early. Once you are the target of a child abuse investigation, document everything as it's been described in earlier chapters. When your rights are violated (and they will be), the first thing you must do is notify the offenders of the specific violations in writing, sent registered/certified mail, and give them a specific period of time to correct those violations, maybe three days. You decide. If they fail to correct those violations, then immediately file a Title 42 lawsuit in Federal court, asking the judge to order the agents of the state to stop these violations. You are not asking for money yet because you have not incurred any damages yet, but why wait until you're in a defensive position? Take the offense and you may not have to lose your children. If the agents of the state continue to violate your civil rights, the court will be in a position to sanction them. A federal lawsuit is pretty scary, even to agents of the state, especially if you know how to use it properly. To wait is to lose.

Child abuse investigations are uniformly based on the gross violation of individual and parental rights coupled with outright fraud. In their arrogance, the agents of the state don't even try to hide their illegal activities as they bluff and bluster their way into your home. If you want to recover damages, you must be prepared to document every illegal action with the intent of using it against them in court. This is where your recorded incidents, your registered letters, your trusted advocates, and your affidavits come in handy.

According to some lawyers, one of the keys to a successful Title 42 lawsuit to recover damages involves dissociating the immune person from their official position within the government. It is their official position that gives them the alleged immunity. However, the government cannot act to violate a person's rights without breaking the law. But if a person, in their official capacity within the government violates your rights, they are acting outside the law and therefore, lose their immunity as a government official.

This is often done by going to Title 18 of the United State Code, Chapter 13 - Civil Rights, sec. 241, "Conspiracy against rights" and sec. 242, "Deprivation of rights under color of law." These sections define the criminal activities associated with the violation of your civil rights. This association demonstrates that the individuals in question acted outside their authority and outside the law by using their official capacity to act under the color of law and with the force of law. They do this when they show up wearing their guns and badges, flaunting their official titles and the power of the state; attempting to bully you into complying with their illegal demands associated with their unfounded allegations. Failing to get your compliance, they do what they want anyway, without probable cause or due process. And they get away with it. But only if you let them.

There are several assumptions you have to make:

1) Many of these agents of the state have taken an oath of office. This oath is generally on file. The ones who have taken this oath, and who have violated your rights, have perjured their oath of office. This is a felony under 18 U.S.C. sec 1621 and proves they acted without lawful authority. If the oath of office is not on file, they are acting outside the authority of the state, and any action taken by them is unsupported by statute.

This oath may or may not vary, but states something to the effect of:

> "I do solemnly swear by the ever living God, that I will support the Constitution of the United States and the State of ____ and faithfully perform the duties of the office of ___ upon which I am about to enter."

Additionally, all lawyers (this includes prosecutors and judges) must take an oath to the bar such as:

"I do solemnly swear by the ever living God that, I

> will support the Constitution of the United States and the Constitution of the State of ___; . . .: I will not counsel or maintain any suit or proceeding which shall appear to me to be without merit or to be unjust: ...: I will employ for the purpose of maintaining the causes confided to me such means only as are consistent with truth and honor: I will never seek to mislead the Judge or jury by any misstatement or false statement of fact or law:. . . I will at all times faithfully and diligently adhere to the [state] Rules of Professional Conduct."

Every state has Rules of Professional Conduct which prosecutors and judges violate frequently in child abuse trials. Get a copy of these rules from your law library and use them to prove perjury of their oath of office. Their participation in and their failure to prevent or correct the violations of your constitutional rights perjures their oath of office. Their prosecuting you without due process or probable cause is also perjury of their oath of office.

2) If an agent of the state isn't required to take an oath of office, chances are his supervisor is. Someone, somewhere, up the chain of command has taken an oath of office. That someone is responsible for the actions of the persons under him, and is presumed to be cognizant of their actions, and in the absence of his intervention to stop those actions, approves of them. You must be sure he receives your notification of the violations of your rights, and give him the opportunity to correct or prevent those violations. If he fails to take action, he will have perjured his oath of office. Name him in the lawsuit.

3) Having more than one person involved in the violation of your rights, you have established a conspiracy. A conspiracy does not require that all parties be in communication regarding the conspiracy, simply that all parties acted in concert to commit the violation of

your rights, regardless of their knowledge of the actions of any other conspirators.

4) Officers of the law, officers of the court, lawyers, and social workers are presumed to have extensive knowledge of the law, thereby establishing that they have knowledge of the violation of your rights. This knowledge is proven by virtue of their oath of office, which automatically gives them a high standard of the law. Social workers, by virtue of their professional position are also expected and presumed to have a high standard of the law, because their job is to protect children under the law. All these agents of the state operating in their official capacity to deprive you of your rights under the color of law and with the force of law, severs them from their immunity. Name each and every party who has participated in or had knowledge of the actions taken to deprive you of your rights and who neglected to prevent or correct the violations, individually in your lawsuit. Name them by their names, and include their title which will verify they acted under the color of law without the authority of law. This includes supervisors who had knowledge of the actions (because you notified these supervisors of the violations) taken by their subordinates who didn't stop them from violating your rights.

This leads to another criminal offense, 18 U.S.C. sec 4, Misprision of a Felony. When your civil rights are violated, it is a felony as described later. When you notify everyone that a felony is occurring, someone is required by law to notify "some judge or other person in civil or military authority under the United States." Failure to notify is Misprision of a Felony. You can notify the court, via your Title 42 lawsuit, that such a felony is occurring, that the named people have knowledge of this felony (including the prosecutor) and failed to notify a judge, etc. You are now in the position of practicing the "manure principle." Find as many charges and counts of charges as possible to stack on your adversaries.

5) Having established that the agents of the state acted outside the law, chances are good you can prove malice, fraud, negligence, and any number of other willfully malicious motives behind their actions, especially if you have documented all the times you notified them of their violations against you and your family and they continued to prosecute. This is icing on the cake used to recover punitive damages and your lawyer's fees.

6) It is safe to assume there is fraud perpetrated by Social Services against the federal government. You just have to find it. We'll address what to do with this later in this chapter under Title 31.

7) Are the statutes cited by the agents of the state constitutional? Maybe so, maybe not, but chances are the court doesn't even care if they are unconstitutional. If they are constitutional, or construed to be constitutional, chances are they were applied unconstitutionally. This would be a violation of your rights. You need to know the statutes and the associated annotations to make a credible allegation.

The point is, that while the agents of the state want you to believe that as an alleged child abuser you have no rights, you can see that the law does not support this. You have all the rights that any other person has. But what good does it do to have these rights if you don't really know what they are and if you are not going to firmly assert them? You must also understand that in order to collect monetary damages, you must first suffer injury.

This probably means that in spite of all you do to protect your rights and your family, the state may take your children anyway. You may have to go to trial. You may suffer severe emotional pain and humiliation and sheer terror at the prospect of going to jail. You will lose the companionship and affection of your children while they are out of your home.

Your children may suffer traumatic examinations and psychological testing. They will certainly suffer emotionally. Some even get suicidal. Some are abused while under the care of the state. Nothing good comes of this kind of unnecessary intervention.

You cannot regain your peace of mind, your family's lost time together. You cannot ever completely heal the pain and trauma. You will probably never again trust the government. But you can hit them where it hurts; in the wallet. You can hold each responsible and knowledgeable party personally and criminally liable. You can bankrupt them. You can cost them their jobs. Maybe you can even put them in jail. It will probably be the only way that you, personally, can make the agents of the state act within the intent and limits of the law.

So far we have used Title 18 sec 241 and 242 of the United States Code to establish that the agents of the state have acted outside their legal authority which severs them from immunity. You add perjury of their oath of office (18 U.S.C. sec 1621), as described earlier, as another criminal act, and Misprision of a Felony (18 U.S.C. sec 4). These criminal accusations open the door for your Title 42 sec. 1986, 1985 and 1983 civil lawsuit. You should include all criminal charges with the civil charges on your complaint. Bear in mind that there are often different approaches to a Title 42 civil rights lawsuit, and the actual technique may vary from person to person. It is your responsibility to do your own research, even if you hire a lawyer, to insure you have the best chances of prevailing.

The problem is that most lawyers won't touch a Title 42 case on a contingency basis. Even when you pay the thousands of dollars they demand for pursuing this case, you'll probably not get the type of representation you expect. You see, this lawyer must play the game by the rules established by the court, because he has to appear before the court again and again. He needs to preserve an amicable working relationship with the court in order to keep practicing law. He is restrained by his oath to the bar, and his need to preserve his standing with the court. He'll represent his own best interests and the court's, not yours. Besides, he'll tell you, these cases are very hard to win. I might add, by lawyers. However, there is an erratic but respectable amount of success reported by pro se litigants. This success has been measured in two ways:

1) Many of these cases have been settled without ever going to court to the satisfaction of the plaintiffs.

2) Many have settled for substantial sums of money. How much money? In most cases, we can only speculate based on lifestyle changes, because there is usually a gag order associated with the agreement. The state knows these settlements have to be kept secret because if they became public, the agents of the state would have to stop doing what they've been doing or else fork over big bucks every time they violated someone's rights. I'd be sure that if there was a gag order, they'd have to pay dearly to buy my silence, and then only for a limited time.

I have heard of one Title 42 action, initiated by a pro se litigant, which settled out of court for $42 million, no gag order attached. This particular person happens to be a member of a law club, Right Way l.a.w., which has done much to perfect Title 42 lawsuits. Its members share their knowledge and their successful techniques with the other members through seminars, tapes, books, and study guides. You must bear in mind, though, that different courts react differently. There is no guarantee that what was successful in one court will be successful in your court.

The reason I mention this club is because if you are going to file a Title 42 lawsuit, you may have to do it without a lawyer. You'll need some help to get started. There are many ways to go about getting that help. While this prospect can be frightening, it can also be advantageous. How's that, you ask? Don't you remember? Lawyers are part of the system.

Think about it. Who knows more about your case than you? You also have the advantage of having nothing to lose, you can fight harder than any lawyer would. Finally, pro se litigants do win Title 42 lawsuits.

But, if you are going to do it yourself, you'll have your work cut out for you. You must know the law, and the rules of civil procedure, and numerous other esoteric legal formalities. If you don't do it right, your case will be thrown out. Michael Brown, radio talk show host and author of "The Irwin Rommel School of Law," says you can spend several hours every night for thirty days in a law library and know the law as well as any lawyer. As you can see, it involves many, many hours of research and study. You will have to make the determination if you are up to it.

You can find law libraries in every city. If there is a courthouse, there is a law library, and if it is tax funded, the public has the right to have access to that library. Law schools have excellent law libraries. Your public library may or may not have one, depending on its size. And, you can access basic legal information on the Internet.

As you proceed with your studies, you'll find it's not as confusing or scary as you have probably been lead to believe. There is no great mystery to understanding the law, and being able to use it to your advantage. If you decide to go for it, don't be intimidated. But don't make the mistake of underestimating how much work is involved.

You should also realize, that without a lawyer to represent you, it is unlikely that you will be taken seriously. This can present a forbidding obstacle and you must be strong enough and knowledgeable enough to stand against the legal assaults that will be hurled against you. The opposition will file numerous motions to dismiss and if you don't know how to respond in a timely and effective manner, you may not even get your day in court.

You will need to learn how to handle the most common complaint of those who file a Title 42 lawsuit: The court dismisses the case. But if the case is dismissed, that is a denial of due process as guaranteed under the constitution, and that can be reversed.

Finally, if the case does get heard, it is quite likely that you will need to file an appeal. Once again, you will be required to know exactly how and when to do this or risk losing the case.

As you can see, representing yourself, or if you prefer, being yourself before the court requires extensive legal research and study to obtain the required knowledge. Even then, you can blow some minor rule and risk losing the case. However you decide to handle it, you will have to weigh the advantages and disadvantages for yourself. No matter what, you will have the advantage of being in the right, and this sincerity and honesty can go quite far in tipping the scales in your favor, assuming you get an honest judge.

It is only fair to warn you, the odds are against getting an honest judge. You'll be able to tell pretty quickly by his rulings. If he doesn't protect your rights, then the universal advice has been to attack him hard and fast. Most people who have been battling the system for years have said the one thing they would do differently is to immediately hold the judges accountable for their actions in court.

This again means filing a Title 42 (and related Title 18 sections) action in Federal court. You are not asking for money in this case, or even pressing criminal charges, but you want a legal remedy against the offending judge. All you want is an honest judge who will rule fairly.

Whether the lawsuit fails or not, you should also mount a legislative attack against the judge. Demand that your congressman get that bad judge impeached, or you will ruin his next reelection campaign. Then keep your promise. Unless he gets the judge impeached, work your tail off to defeat him during the next election. Congressmen serve only two year terms. When he is defeated, make the same demand of his replacements, until the offending judge is impeached. Maybe the next judge will get the message. These bad judges must have their careers destroyed, each and every one of them who violate the law and the constitution, as a warning to other judges who would follow suit.

UNORTHODOX BUT IT SEEMS TO WORK

Any lawyer will scoff at what I'm going to talk about in this section. However, I believe that if I give you all the information that I've found, you can make your own determination about how you want to proceed. This is a very brief description of a new style of Title 42 lawsuit being used for the past year by members of Right Way l.a.w. It is only fair to warn you that some of this information has been labeled by certain people as "patriot mythology" and Right Way l.a.w. is sometimes referred to as "wrong way law." I have personally interviewed the people at Right Way, and have examined extensive amounts of their material. They have spent many years in the trial and error method of standing up for their rights in our courts, and have begun to perfect some of their techniques.

I have compared their court filings with those of lawyers. I have compared the results and found that lawyers spend a lot more time involved with these filings than Right Way members do on theirs. Being that these are two different approaches to the same type of lawsuit, the only way I can measure success is in the ultimate outcome. Right Way members cases' have been declared as dismissed, yet they continue to move forward and the dismissal is effectively invalidated. Can lawyers make the same claim? Right Way members' cases are not successfully disputed on the rules or points of law, and they create some interesting confusion among the lawyers who must defend against their cases.

This confusion arises from the premise that there are two separate and distinct United States governments. This very strange assertion is supported by Title 31 of the Code of Federal Regulations, 31 C.F.R. Ch.1 (7-1-89 Edition) Monetary Offices, Treasury, Part 51 and Part 52. In comparing Parts 51 and 52, there are two separate definitions of a state, both valid and operating simultaneously. One definition (Part 51.2) refers to the body politic generally defined as the democracy and refers to the 50 (capital "S") State governments. The other definition (Part 52.2) refers to the body politic generally defined as the republic under the constitution and refers to the government of any of the 50 (small "s") states. Why is this distinction defined in the code if it is not important?

Their main contention is that because there are two different bodies politic, and because our courts today presume that all people are operating under the (capital "S") State (the democracy), that if they properly rebut that presumption and define their court and its rules under Article III of the constitution, they can invoke a constitutional court. From there, anything done by the (capital "S") State court is not within the jurisdiction of their Article III court and is simply refused for fraud because it doesn't comply with the rules defined and agreed upon at the time the suit was filed. If the court did not agree to the rules, it would not have accepted the filing, therefore it agreed by default.

Surprisingly, these suits are not being thrown out of court. They cannot be dismissed because that provision has been expressly denied in the rules of the suit. They are operating under an ancient principle from the Magna Carta, "The suit of the sovereign creates the court." They seem to have created a court that the opposing lawyers don't know how to deal with and have been somewhat successfully reasserting their constitutional protections.

Will these new suits be more successful than the old style Title 42 suits? It's too soon to tell, but it looks very promising. I can tell you that Right Way members have definitely done their research, the same as any lawyer, and they are playing by the rules as is evidenced by the courts' responses.

There is no way that I can give enough detail here to set you on the right path for this technique. My intention was to provide you with all the options, and let you make your own decisions. If you are interested in either traditional pro se techniques as taught by Mike Brown or the more unorthodox techniques as espoused by Right Way l.a.w., you will find both resources listed in the appendix

DEFRAUDING THE FEDERAL GOVERNMENT

"There is a reckoning coming. God has sent soldiers to deal with the problem. Actual trained soldiers to deal with the problem . . . When you send soldiers to deal with something, they usually prosecute a war. This is a war of litigation and legislation. If I can litigate you guys into jail, I'll do it. If I can legislate you out of business, I'll do it." Mike Neligh, Coalition of Parents

There is an organization, The Coalition of Parents, who have a requirement for membership: you or an immediate family member must have been falsely accused of child abuse. This is not a support group, or a group that puts on seminars or training. They are not about educating the public. They state it is a waste of time to try to educate anyone who hasn't been falsely accused of child abuse, because most people don't believe it actually happens to innocent people.

The Coalition of Parents is a highly disciplined and focused group of people whose sole objective is to expose the massive fraud perpetrated by the individual states against the Federal Government and in so doing, bankrupt the state. They are not right wing, left wing, liberal or conservative. They don't take sides. They are only interested in the truth. If an individual filing a Title 42 action is guerilla warfare, then this organization is fighting the war on the front lines with the latest high tech weaponry available. Using military tactics, they conduct strategic operations against the corrupt child abuse industry under the False Claims Act, Title 31 sections 3729 and 3730. Their motto is "Litigate, Publicize, Legislate."

According to Mike Neligh, founder of The Coalition of Parents, the child protection system is a money making scheme. In order to perpetuate this monster, 3,000 children a day must be removed from their homes. This was relatively easy to do when the child protection scam began, by targeting minority, low income families and welfare moms. This group of people was accustomed to being victimized and they garnered little sympathy from the rest of America when their children were taken away. They weren't accustomed to fighting for their rights, and willingly submitted to whatever the state ordered them to do.

Since 1987, the child savers started running out of people. There weren't enough children already in the system to keep the system going. They had to expand their operations to include working Americans. Obviously, they cannot muster 3,000 valid cases of child abuse a day, so they must invent abuse and neglect. At first, the definition of child abuse was commonly understood to be obvious injury or severe neglect resulting in injury to the child.

Today, you can be charged with abuse or neglect simply for yelling at your child, or spanking, or for home-schooling. This deviation from common sense has become necessary to expand the types of abuse so that more children can be swept into the system.

On the average, each child in foster care is worth $22,000 to the state. However, if the state can have that child diagnosed or declared a special needs child, the amount can jump as high as $250,000 per child per year or more. This money comes from the federal government in the form of Medicaid/Medicare and other federal funds from as many as a thousand different federal programs, even including such agencies as NASA and the Dept. of Transportation. This stolen money supports an entire industry; the child protection industry, and provides easy income to state approved therapists, doctors, hospitals, group homes, psychiatrists, teachers, etc. as well as state and county departments of social services.

Some of the simplest examples of fraud involve unneeded medical attention. Many times the parents are billed for this treatment, and another bill is sent to the federal government as a Medicaid/Medicare claim. The same thing goes for foster care, the parents are billed and so is the federal government. There are variations on this scam and there are many more devious methods used.

For example: Many times, to make the child compliant, they will use drugs like Ritalin and Zoloft to sedate the child, completely unconcerned about the fact that they precipitated the child's emotional problems by removing the child from his parents. This creates a "special needs" child. Special needs children generate enormous amounts of money for the state.

There are documented cases where agents of the state have tried experimental psychological techniques to make a young child regress into infancy in an attempt to break the child's bond with his real parents and force him to reattach emotionally to his foster parents. This has been done by putting the child (as old as five years old!) back on the bottle and refusing to allow the child to walk, forcing him to crawl, among other abusive and humiliating techniques. These experiments fail dismally and damage a child's psychology permanently.

There are documented cases where the state misrepresents the race of the child. For example: claiming the child is American Indian when he isn't, thereby getting extra federal funds allocated specifically for American Indian children that they are not entitled to. There are also documented incidents of young children "enrolled" in federal job training programs and moneys being disbursed from NASA for fraud associated with child protection. With so many programs available, it is impossible to imagine what a devious mind could come up with.

There's $500 billion of fraud perpetrated against the federal government each year. Each state has been responsible for defrauding the federal government out of billions of dollars. That's billions of dollars per state! The Coalition of Parents is uncovering this fraud and bringing it to the attention of the Attorney General. The AG can decide to prosecute the case, giving the whistle blower 10% of the recovered money as a reward, or decline to prosecute. If the AG declines, then the whistleblower can sue the state on behalf of the United States government and keep 25% to 33% of the recovered money.

The Coalition of Parents is doing this with a clearly defined plan of action. Since this is a fairly new area of litigation, and there is little existing case law, they are out to establish the case law in their favor. They recommend that individuals do not mess up the case law by attempting this independently. In fact they say if they catch you doing it pro se, they'll interfere with your attempt because you'd mess it up. Title 31 actions are strictly and solely dependant on how well the investigation is done. They would rather that individuals contact them with their evidence, and let them put their expert team to work. Their team consists of the best experts in their respective fields of law, private investigations, government accounting methods and public relations. All are ex-military. All have obtained the best results in their respective fields.

They take a single documentable lie; a lie that is proven in the paperwork, and conduct an investigation based on that information. Some of these lies, repeated over and over with other hapless families, have turned out to reveal several billion dollars in fraud. In addition to recovering the amount of money the government was defrauded out of, there is a fine of $10,000 per occurrence (per lie) and three times the damages.

They have two goals. The first is to force the states to be honest. The second is to stop the federal money: they want to stop the government from paying a bounty for children.

According to Neligh, the bottom line is this: "The Coalition of Parents wants the people who are working for the system who can't be jailed to be fired. They want the records burned, the buildings torn down and the ground under them salted so that nothing like it grows up in a good long time."

The threshold for political clout is a paid membership list of 100,000. The Coalition of Parents wants to increase its membership to gain this clout. With 100,000 members and a couple of lawsuits under its belt, they believe they can get the federal funds stopped. When the federal funds are stopped, there will be no money to fund the abuses by the system so the abuses will stop. Keep in mind, they will not be diverted from their goal, and will not expend their money or energy in any other endeavor.

APPEARING BEFORE A GRAND JURY

Right Way members have successfully petitioned the court for an appointment to appear before a grand jury in their Article III court. This is a major victory, and it means that we have regained a long-lost recourse against the lawless elements of the children's protection system. Their petition is based on the same format as their constitutional lawsuits, and the court cannot seem to find any reason to deny them their petition. Until now, it has been virtually impossible for an ordinary citizen to appear before a Grand Jury and present evidence of criminal activity. It has always been up to the prosecutor to do it, and prosecutors will not target the Department of Social

Services.

If you have gathered evidence of criminal activities by any agents of the state, you can present that evidence before a grand jury and ask for an indictment. Then those agents will have to face criminal prosecution for their crimes. Be prepared for a fight from the prosecutor. You might have to teach the Grand Jury about its actual power and authority, if they'll listen. It's kind of a happy occurrence of 'what goes around, comes around.' Contact Right Way l.a.w. for more details.

If you do appear before a grand jury, be sure to have all of your evidence compiled and witnesses available. You don't want to waste your attempt because you weren't prepared. No doubt the prosecutor will pooh-pooh your evidence, so it had better be tight and complete. He will be in the Grand Jury room after you have left, so make your presentation good.

CHAPTER 12

CHANGE THE LAW

"What we obtain too cheap, we esteem too lightly: 'Tis dearness only that gives every thing its value. Heaven knows how to put a proper price upon its goods; and it would be strange indeed, if so celestial an article as FREEDOM should not be highly rated." Thomas Paine

One of the primary causes of false allegations of child abuse, aside from the federal money it generates for the state, is the vague definitions of abuse, including such things as mental abuse, bruising, and neglect.

These terms, being incorporated into most state statutes are poorly defined, if at all, and leave the determination of abuse up to a case worker or police officer. This is not an objective application of the law, but rather, a subjective determination based on the personal biases of the person making the determination. This clearly makes it an unconstitutional law, for lack of being specific.

For example, a case worker is charged with making the assessment of abuse against a child. She does this with no first hand knowledge of the child's temperament or personality, no post graduate training in human psychology, no first had knowledge of the social dynamics or normal interaction of the family unit in question, no idea of the child's particular emotional and intellectual strengths and weaknesses, and no knowledge of the child's physiology. She knows nothing about the parents' parenting techniques, their values, their goals, or the factors leading up to the incident that was reported. Based on only an anonymous tip from another person without such knowledge, she must decide if this child has been abused.

What if the child is hypersensitive and cries easily? Emotional abuse.

What if he bruises easily? Physical abuse.

What if he has a medical condition that precipitates injury such as a seizure disorder or Osteogenesis Imperfecta? Physical abuse.

What if the child is normally clumsy, falling and crashing into things all the time, and gets a bump on his head? Physical abuse.

What if the parents home school? Educational neglect.

What if he was a low birth weight baby who is being breast-fed, who doesn't gain weight fast enough to suit the doctor, even though he stays within the normal growth curve for his birth weight, and the mother refuses to put him on formula? Neglect.

What if the child is a teenage girl who just wants to get even with a strict step-dad? Sexual abuse.

The possibilities are unlimited for the case worker to make an entirely subjective assessment of abuse, without a shred of empirical evidence to support the allegation.

Supposedly, there are laws in place to prevent abuses by the system, but these laws have no teeth, and are easily undermined. The Child Abuse and Neglect Accountability Act of 1993 supposedly makes it impossible for states to get Federal grant money if they do not enact laws making it a criminal offense for a person to make a report of child abuse or neglect without having a reasonable belief that the report is true. It also requires that states provide for penalties if someone intentionally causes or persuades a child to make an allegation of child abuse or neglect without having a reasonable belief that such an allegation is true. The drawback to this law is that it must be proven that the person making the report did so with the *intent* to expose another person to public hatred, contempt, ridicule, criminal investigation, or to gain advantage in a civil proceeding. If this intent cannot be proven, then they can make a report with so-called *absolute immunity* from prosecution or civil recourse. Intent is almost impossible to prove.

New York state has presented a bill[24] that would put some teeth into the law. Basically it states that the Social Services department is required to maintain the records of unfounded child abuse reports. They must notify the victim of the unfounded report within thirty days that the report was unfounded, and inform them of the right to pursue criminal prosecution for falsely reporting child abuse. They also have the right to possess the record, and the record cannot be expunged without consent of the victim. The key word in this law is **unfounded**. This eliminates the burden of proving intent, and appears to rest instead on the actual evidence. This is clearly a step in the right direction.

OBJECTIVE, AGE-APPROPRIATE DEFINITION OF ABUSE

The assessment of abuse must be removed from the realm of subjective determination. There must be an objective, age-appropriate definition of child abuse. One key factor in this definition is that the definition of injury should not be construed to include minor bruising on the child's bottom.

Medically speaking, the bottom is well protected against injury, it is not covering any vital organs and is

---

[24] Introduced in Assembly January 31, 1995. An act to amend the social services law.

well padded with muscle and fat. It is perfectly designed for administering a spanking without danger of injury.

Bruising is not a serious injury unless there is a medical problem which makes it so, and then only in rare cases. Neither is there need for massive black and blue marks on the bottom of a two-year-old, nor even a ten-year-old for that matter. Naturally, broken skin or blistering, which could lead to infection, isn't necessary either. Welts, which are often gasped at by the manipulative child savers, are transitory, sometimes turning into minor bruises, usually simply fading away within hours. Your hand can leave finger shaped welts on a sensitive bottom, without your having been abusive during the spanking.

My Eric bruised easily, which always caused me concern when we spanked him, not because of any supposed injury, but because of the mood of the state regarding bruising. If he was to be spanked hard enough to make an impression on his attitude, he'd often develop a small bruise or two on his bottom. However, this was not the case with Jacob who was older and got spanked harder. How can the state account for this kind of a variable?

Perhaps with a standard measure of injury; after the age of reason, say five or six, you could use the child's hand as a measure of the extent of bruising on the bottom. If his hand can cover the bruise, it's not abuse. Smaller hands would mean smaller bruised areas. This can satisfy the objective definition of abuse in the context of age appropriate discipline, yet we would not be charging anyone with child abuse for what certainly is not a major or life threatening injury.

I've witnessed legislators struggle with this issue only to simply drop it because they lacked the wisdom or integrity to address this difficult definition. Our representatives are terrified of bad publicity, and will compromise anything to prevent it, including parents' rights. They don't want to be seen as condoning anything that could be maliciously construed as injuring a child, even if it is a false representation. They don't have the courage to right the wrongs being perpetrated by their own laws. The problem is that on a healthy child, a small bruise is nothing more than a minor discoloration. If bruising really was a serious injury, then we should, by the logic of the child savers, be rushing our children to the doctor each time they fall down and bump themselves. Children will recover quickly from minor bruising. They won't recover from ineffective discipline techniques.

Changing the law to allow minor bruising on the bottom is probably the only way to stop the agents of the state from taking children away from parents who spank. They are vehemently opposed to spanking and they'll take children who don't even have bruises. The law must state unequivocally that parents may spank their children, and that minor bruising on the bottom is not an injury by the definition of child abuse.

In Colorado, a petite step-mom reached up and slapped her smart-mouthed, five foot ten inch, 160 pound stepson across the face and was charged with child abuse. This was pure foolishness. Any child who is adult sized shouldn't be able to go crying to social services simply because he receives a well-deserved slap in the face. Hitting with a closed fist is probably not a good idea. Slap the face? Why not? Where's the injury? That is the issue after all, if there is no injury, there can be no child abuse. Injury is the issue. Make sure that is clear in the law.

Having determined that injury is the issue, injury must be clearly defined, and objectively measurable. Today, humiliation to the child is considered emotional injury. I consider it an effective training tool, used selectively. Look at the effects of peer pressure.

But selective humiliation is distinctly different from constantly belittling a child or deliberately causing psychological trauma. Emotional abuse must be defined as causing measurable injury to be considered abuse. This means the long term effects must be obvious and measurable before the charges can be leveled. Right now the determination is entirely subjective, and left in the hands of emotional non-experts.

ACCOUNTABILITY, CIVIL LIABILITY

Another legislative change that must be made is to make all agents of the state accountable, under statute, for the damaging actions they perpetrate against non-abusive parents. These laws should make them personally liable for attorney's fees for defendants that are found not guilty. They should also be liable for criminal charges and for monetary damages in civil lawsuits, and put their jobs at risk, for instances involving incompetence, negligence, malice, or fraud. These laws should include the concept that they "knew or reasonably should have known" they were acting outside their stated objective to protect a genuinely abused or neglected child, or outside the authority of the law.

Parents should also have the right to collect damages in a civil lawsuit if the allegations were unfounded or found to be fabricated, with or without the knowledge of the agent of the state, and the agent continued the investigation in spite of the lack of evidence of abuse or neglect. If the parents' names remain on the state registry, they should be allowed civil recourse.

ELIMINATE ABSOLUTE IMMUNITY, ANONYMITY

Eliminate the immunities the agents of the state

and people who report allegations of child abuse enjoy. Hold them to the same "knew or reasonably should have known" standard of actions as everyone else. Make them personally liable for all damages caused by their false allegations, and for all unwarranted investigations and intrusions into non-abusive families. Make them subject to punitive damages the same as any other negligent or malicious act. Eliminate anonymous reporting.

TRIAL BY JURY TO REMOVE CHILDREN FROM THE HOME

The legislators should require a trial by jury in all cases involving the removal of the child from the home. In the case of an emergency placement, this trial should occur within 24 hours of the removal of the child. Make social services prove to the jury exactly how they tried to keep the family intact and exactly how the child is in imminent danger. This would mean that they must collect their evidence and prepare their case before they can whisk the children out of the home. Social workers and judges have an incestuous relationship, and this jury requirement would eliminate their virtually invincible control over helpless families.

While we're at it, allow juries for all family court trial, the same as any other civil trial. This will go a long way to stop the abuses by the system.

INVESTIGATIONS CONDUCTED BY LAW ENFORCEMENT, NOT SOCIAL SERVICES

Remove all child abuse investigations from the realm of social services. Child abuse should be treated as a crime and investigated by the appropriate law enforcement agency. Police are trained in evidence collection and solving crimes. Social workers aren't. In the cases where intervention is required, have private agencies who are publicly accountable, provide counseling, family intervention, foster care, etc.

ADVISE THE CHILD OF HIS LIABILITY IF HE LIES

Currently, children are never told of their potential for criminal prosecution if they make a false accusation. Our legislators should pass a law requiring that all people who are mandated to report child abuse inform the child of the legal consequences if he is lying about the accusation if he comes to them to accuse someone. Crystal, a young girl who made a false accusation against her father, admitted that if she had been told that she could get in trouble for lying about her accusation, would not have accused her dad. She claims she was encouraged to accuse her dad by the people she told her story to, who just happened to be mandated reporters.

CHILD PROTECTION WORKERS SHOULD BE PARENTS

Require that all social workers working for the government who handle children's issues be themselves parents. This requirement alone could go far toward preventing knee-jerk, hysterical reactions to innocent statements or outright accusations made by children.

SOCIAL WORKERS/CHILD PROTECTION WORKERS LICENSED AND BONDED

This is a very simple technique for eliminating rabid attacks against law-abiding parents. If all case workers who are hired by any government agency were required by law to be bonded, much like our county commissioners and other public officials are in many areas, they could be held accountable for their illegal actions against families. Only fair and reasonable social workers could qualify to be bonded, the bad ones would have to post their own bond or not get the job. Since they stand to lose their own bond money, it would be a powerful tool to reign in abuses by the system.

The social services field should be regulated by testing, licensing, and a sworn oath. Currently, there are often no specific requirements other than a minimal college degree to be a social worker. Doctors, lawyers, therapists and police officers are all constrained by regulatory requirements designed to monitor and weed out the bad apples. Hold social workers, who have the power to destroy families, to the same high professional standard. If they violate their oath, they can be punished for perjury.

GUARDIAN AD LITEM IMPARTIALITY

Require that anyone who is a Guardian ad Litem should not be sympathetic to the position of the state and should not derive benefit, income, or position from the state. Eliminate the profit motives that protect the interests of the state to the exclusion of the interests of the child. They should also be required to undergo special training to enable them to recognize when a child is influenced by psychological manipulation such Parental Alienation Syndrome and other potentially abusive or isolationist tactics practiced by the agents of the state or hostile parents.

REQUIRE LEGITIMATE INVESTIGATIONS BY GUARDIAN AD LITEM

Require that Guardians ad Litem conduct bona fide investigations on behalf of the child instead of giving lip service to the investigation. The results of these investigations must be made available to all parties involved. Make the falsification of this investigative report punishable by mandatory fine and imprisonment.

PARENTAL REPRESENTATION DURING QUESTIONING, MANDATORY RECORDING OF CHILDREN'S STATEMENTS

Make it mandatory that all questioning of children by school personnel, social workers, police, and other agents of the state be recorded and that a representative of the family must always be present to preclude the possibility of leading questions or misinterpretations. This recording must be available to the parents of the child upon request. Those who have nothing to hide, have nothing to fear.

ELIMINATE SECRECY

Eliminate all requirements for secrecy and sealed records in unfounded cases. Open these records for public inspection so that abuses by the system can be exposed. Make the falsification of any records related to a child abuse investigation punishable by mandatory fine and imprisonment. Once again the standard of "knew or reasonably should have known" should prevail.

ELIMINATE HEARSAY EVIDENCE

All hearsay evidence must be ruled inadmissable during a child abuse trial, whether it is a civil or criminal trial. This is a gross violation of rights, yet it is a common practice in virtually every court in our land. Any evidence presented during a child abuse trial must meet the rules of evidence as required in any other criminal or civil trial. Special care must be taken to allow a defendant the right to present all evidence in his defense, which is often denied in today's family courts.

PROSECUTE THE STATE FOR ABUSE

Many children are intentionally and/or negligently abused while under the care of the state. Some of this abuse is severe. The state must be held to the same standard as private citizens are in this regard. Any agent of the state who neglects to protect, or has knowledge of and fails to prevent or correct the abuse, and/or participates in abusive behavior toward children who are in the custody of the state should be held doubly liable for the abuses perpetrated against those children. If they are taking the children to protect them, then they must be held to the highest standard, and be expected to provide adequate and effective protection against abuse by anyone who comes in contact with them. If they don't, they should be charged criminally or held civilly liable the same as anyone else.

THE RIGHT TO CONFRONT ACCUSER

The sixth amendment to the constitution guarantees the right of the defendant to be confronted with the witnesses against him. Today's child abuse trials do not meet that requirement, many times the child accusers never testify, or if they do, do so via video tape or closed circuit television. I will not dispute the probability that a child testifying in open court, facing her accuser, can be frightening. But so is being falsely charged with child abuse, and maybe a lying child accuser could be shamed into telling the truth by the mere presence of the accused. The only time a child should be allowed to be protected by video testimony is if the accused is actually hostile toward, or intimidating the witness in the courtroom.

JUDGES

Many judges have been ignorantly taught that it is better to err on the side of the safety of the child. By this reasoning it is preferable to put ten innocent people in jail, to destroy ten faultless families, than to let one child abuser go loose. This logic, reminiscent of the dreadful Salem witch trials, has condemned hundreds of thousands of innocent families to family separation, termination of parental rights, bankruptcy, and imprisonment. Judges who will be ruling in child protection cases, both criminal and civil, should be instructed on the ramifications of court-perpetrated child abuse; of the damage caused by invading the privacy of law-abiding families and ripping children from their loving parents arms in the name of child protection. They must also be expected to harshly condemn abusive processes and tactics by the agents of the state.

Yes, I know. This one is highly unlikely.

LOCAL GOVERNMENT

Your county commissioners are usually responsible for the hiring of the Director of Social Services. If your social services department has run amuck, present your documented complaints to them, the more you can gather the better. Bring the press along to the meeting where you present this information to them. Remind them that they are elected officials and are accountable for what their departments under them do. Inform them of their potential liability on the record, and that they have knowledge, and the right duty relationship to prevent or correct the abuses by the system that they have oversight over.

Insist that they review Department of Social Services Policies and Procedures with an eye to correcting the abuses that are occurring. Make them hold the Director of Social Services accountable, and insist they terminate him if he continues to allow his department perpetrate abuses against law-abiding parents and families. If they won't, remember in November.

If your county sheriff's department has participated in these abuses, present your complaints to him also. Inform him that if his department would not use their guns and badges to enforce the abuses of social services, they would be less able to trample the rights of non-abusive parents.

Then tell him that if he will not protect the constitutional rights of the citizens in his county, you will strive to elect someone who will. Then keep your promise to remember in November.

Write letters to the editor. Get your local paper to do a story on the abuses. Get on local talk radio shows as a guest, get on local cable access television, get on the news. Name names. Get as much bad publicity out as possible. Start a grass-roots drive to oust the villains the next election. Go door to door, and tell your community nobody is safe once they're targeted. It's not a liberal or conservative issue, it's not left wing or right wing, it's not about religion. It crosses all political and religious boundaries. It's about parents and children.

City police chiefs fall under the purview of the mayor and/or the city council. All are elected officials who despise bad publicity. This tactic can work on them also.

Some jurisdictions are beginning to establish child protective teams consisting of a representative from each of the government agencies involved and volunteers from the community at large. They regularly review child abuse cases and determine if the public and private agencies involved were in compliance with the law. They also make recommendations regarding further actions, and report to the county whether there were any lapses and inadequacies in the child protection system, and if they have been corrected.

Volunteer to serve on this team, and use your knowledge of the law to rein in the abuses by the state. If your jurisdiction doesn't have provisions for this team, work to get it established. Then serve on it. Get other like-minded parents to serve also. Pack that child protection team with family advocates. Then nail the department of social services every time they violate the law.

PARENTAL RIGHTS AMENDMENT

Colorado recently lost its bid to get a parental rights amendment added to its constitution. A massive advertising campaign, which said this amendment would cause more children to be abused, made many supporters change their minds at the last minute. Your campaign must be persuasive and powerful enough to subvert that devious tactic. Don't be afraid to use emotional appeals. It's not that hard to find children like Crystal who wrote the letter in the following chapter. Crystal is a brave young lady who wants to publicize her plight as much as possible. Think of how much emotional appeal she could have in a well designed television campaign touting the evils of child protection and how it violated her family's rights, and how if she had been protected by a parental rights amendment, she would not have been taken out of her home.

Try all avenues from the ballot initiative to pushing your state representatives to sponsor it as a bill. If at first you don't succeed, try, try again.

OPPOSE PARENTAL LICENSING

There is a movement among the "experts" out there to require parental licensing. The 1997 Minnesota state legislature is reported to be considering a parental licensing bill. At first, such a bill would require that any unlicensed parents be subject to periodic visitations by the agents of the state to determine if the child is being raised "properly." This will most likely include the requirement that the child is being taught the "proper values" and that his "rights as a child" are not infringed upon by repressive parents. It also will provide a vehicle for children to be easily removed from homes where parents do not follow the parenting practices that licensed parents are trained to follow. This will likely mean that home-schooling or spanking will be, in practice, forbidden.

The next step would be legislation to allow the government to take custody of children who are born to unlicensed parents to be adopted by licensed parents. The only way to be licensed would be to take parenting classes (designed by none other than our ubiquitous "experts") and to pass a licensing exam administered by the state.

I believe that the right to raise your child according to your values is one of the non-enumerated rights in the ninth amendment. The government can neither compel someone to become pregnant, nor prevent them from bearing children without forcibly assaulting the mother's body. Only God can do either, only God can choose who to bless with children, and man has no right to second guess God's decisions.

Parental licensing will not reduce child abuse, but it will violate one of our most basic rights. God commanded man to be fruitful and multiply, and built the instinct to procreate into our very essence. Whenever man interferes with God's design, he screws it up.

This idea must be fought vigorously, because even though the child savers may fail on their first attempt, they'll be back until they succeed. That is a promise. This is going to be a long, hard fight, and only you can prevent this obscenity from becoming established as law. If you don't fight it, your children will lose their rights as parents to raise their children according to God's commands. The losers will be your grandchildren. Is that what you want for them?

EPILOGUE

In closing, I'd like to include an unsolicited letter from a young girl who falsely accused her father of sexual abuse. In case there is any doubt on your part that the information I've presented in the book is exaggerated or patently false, just read Crystal's letter. It is published in its original form without any editing.

Hi, my name is Crystal, I am 14 and I've done a terrible thing. I have made the worst mistake in my life. I told a terrible lie, and not only got myself but my family in the biggest nightmare you could ever imagine. At this point in time, I can't believe that I thought this, but I was selfish and I was jealous of my Dad, and I thought he had something I didn't. I wanted my Mom and Dad to get a divorce so that I could have Mom all to myself. I tried for a long time to split them up, without them hardly noticing, by acting up, and causing arguments between them. That didn't seem to work, so I had to make a plan to make something so bad happen that my Mom would leave my Dad. In school they were teaching us about abuse and I thought about telling my counselor that my Dad beat me, but since he didn't and I didn't have any bruises on me I couldn't say that. That is when I hit on sexual abuse. They taught us allot about that in sex-ed at school an I knew what to say about that. I could say just enough to my counselor so that there wouldn't be any physical signs and get my Mom mad enough at Dad so that she would leave him. So I talked to my counselor. She kept telling me that I didn't do anything wrong, and that I wasn't the only one with this problem. She acted as though she was my best friend and immediately believed every word I said. She didn't even ask me any questions. I thought this was great, my lie is going to work. She said she had to call CPS

(Child Protective Services) and someone would come and talk to me about it. Eventually a lady named Corrine came and talked to me. By this time I had my story down pat after telling it to my school counselor. When I saw her she said that she was so worried about me and she told me she was here to help me. I told her my lie. She told me my Dad was sick and needed professional help. She told me about foster care and made it sound all wonderful, and that I wouldn't be held against my will, and I would only be there a very short period of time. I thought that this would give my Mom enough time to get mad at my dad and leave him. They didn't take me that day but I told my Mom about it. My Mom didn't react like I expected though, because she didn't believe me. She said that some of the things I said didn't make sense, because some of the times I said my Dad did things to me, she was either with him, or was watching us. She thought that maybe I misunderstood my Dad showing me normal affection for something else. Anyway, because of this I started to get a little scared that this wasn't going to work and maybe this really wasn't enough to shake her up. The next school day, I went to my counselor and told her that my Dad touched me again (he didn't) and that I wanted to call Corrine. She came to the school to see me and she told me she was going to take me down to Victim Services. In the car she told me that I was going to talk to someone who worked for the police dept. When we got there we went into a room that had a two way mirror and a camcorder on the other side of the mirror. I asked him what the camcorder was for and he said it was so he didn't have to take notes, and that it was confidential between me, Corrine and him. So I told my lie again, but since I didn't have much detail, he started asking me leading questions about things that let me know what he wanted to hear. My lie grew as I figured out what he wanted. Then Corrine said that "SHE" was going to take custody of me. We went to her office and called some foster homes to see where she could put me.

Corrine drove me to the foster home and I started to get scared, but I thought this would shake up Mom enough to divorce my Dad. At that point in time I had NO idea what I had started. After a few days I realized this wasn't working the way I expected and this was NOT what I wanted at all. Not only that but I now knew what I had lost, and how mean I had been to my Dad and realized how much he tried to be a good Dad to me and how much he loved me. My Family was and is the most important thing that I have. I was so lucky that Mom and Dads marriage was so strong, I need them both. I found out that DSS was NOT my friend and that the only people that know what is best for me and who protect me are my Mom and Dad who love me. I had to go to victim services again so that the man there could see how things were going. When I got there I went into the same room with the mirror and camcorder. The man asked me how things were going, and I said awful and told him that I lied about all of this, none of the things I said that my Dad did to me were true. I told him about my plan to make my Mom divorce my Dad and said that wasn't what I wanted now. He said that I have confused things and that people weren't going to know what to believe. After that no one seemed to care about me, they turned their backs on me. No one would talk to me. Now I had no one at all. I was so alone and scared, I couldn't talk to my Mom or Dad because they wouldn't let me. They didn't even know where I was. After a couple more days they finally let me see my Mom. I just broke down when I saw her and all I could say was that I was so sorry, tell Dad I am so sorry. Then after talking to Mom I found out that the police were trying to put Dad in jail and they were using that tape they made that was supposed to be confidential. I also found out that DSS basically owned me now they had taken custody of me in court. They didn't tell me about any of this; I didn't have a clue that all this was going to happen. I had discovered that DSS was EVIL and all they wanted to do is break up my family and put my Dad in jail. They lied to me to get me to say things that weren't true on video just so they could break up my family and have control over me. I hate them. They said they were "protecting" me but now I feel so unsafe and scared. They are the ones who I need to be protected from. Since I have been in foster care, I have seen and heard things I could have never imagined. I was in a room with another girl who was really abused, and I could see for the first time why my parents tried to teach me things they did, and how lucky I was to have a kind, gentle Daddy I had and that my Mom and Dad being together was really GOOD for me, and that we need to be together as a strong family.

Well, for the past 4 weeks we have been in therapy. It has been a total waste of time. They are supposed to be getting to the bottom of this but all they want is Dad to take a polygraph lie detector test to "prove" that he didn't do anything. Dad, my Mom and me are all telling them exactly the same story, it seems that they just cannot handle the truth, that none of what I lied about happened. They haven't been able to prove anything that I said in my lie, but if they would look, and ask the right questions they would find that I lied and my Dad would NEVER do anything like that to me. They are making him out to be guilty and have to prove himself innocent. I didn't know that was the way our country worked; as far as I am concerned it isn't. I lied. My Dad did nothing, yet he is the one who is being blamed for this. It isn't fair. They said to my Mom and Dad that they shouldn't want me home because I might do this again, and they are doing anything to keep our family ripped apart. They told me that even if my Dad passes the polygraph lie detector that I would have to stay in foster care until they could find out that my Dad wasn't going to slap me around or throw something at me because he was mad at me. That made me VERY angry because I know my Dad forgives me and has never hit anyone in anger or for any other reason. They had No reason to say that to me. These therapists say they are so good at getting to the bottom of things, but they are dragging their feet on this like you wouldn't believe, and they don't care. They are just playing a game with us and this is my family, this is NOT a game.

This Christmas I got to stay at my home with my Mom and my Brother because my foster family was going out of state. BUT my DAD had to leave because I was there and I didn't get to spend the holidays with him, and that's what hurt the most. I need to tell my Dad I am sorry for all the hurt I brought on him. I need to hear him say that he forgives me for the horrible things I have done. But they won't let me. I guess it would interfere with their "plan" to keep our family apart. Today I have to go back to the foster home, and I will be back in isolation.

I can't change what I did, but I can make things better in the future. I know that if they did this to me, they have and will do this to other children and their families and I want to do anything to stop them!!!!!

But first, I want to go home to my family. Please, if anyone can help me call my Mom and Dad . This thing is such a monster that we can't handle it on our own. They tell me I have no legal rights to do anything about this. I can't believe that is true. Please Please help me. I am scared about what is going to happen and I need your help.

Yours truly,

Crystal S.

APPENDIX

RESOURCES:

National Child Abuse Defense & Resource Center
PO Box 638
Holland, OH 43528
Phone: (419)865-0513
Fax: (419)865-0526

> "Working with criminal defense and civil court lawyers where allegations of abuse have been made along with persons falsely accused of abuse."
>
> This all-volunteer organization is strictly a resource center to assist in the defense of false allegations of child abuse. They offer books, articles, audio & video tapes, and psychiatric treatises and studies to aid the defense lawyer or the falsely accused defendant. They also can refer you to a good attorney who can effectively defend you if you are falsely accused.

Coalition of Parents
Phone: (800)478-9410
Phone: (907)345-9701
Fax: (907)345-9862
Internet Address:
http://www.customcpu.com/personal/mneligh/cop
http://www.customcpu.com/personal/mneligh/cop/mission.htm
http://www.isc.org/men/orgs/blurb/com.html
I also suggest you do a net search under [coalition of

parents], you'll be amazed at what you'll find.

Dedicated to exposing the fraud against the Federal Government associated with the child protection system, and seeking recovery in the courts. Prerequisite of membership: you must have been falsely accused of child abuse.

The Coalition of Parents is advocating forming an umbrella over other organizations like AFN, CCLA, FMSF, FREE, VOCAL and others prevent duplication of efforts and lend nationwide fundraising ability.

The Irwin Rommel School of Law
Peter Jon Simpson
c/o 4842 N. Magnolia
Chicago, Illinois 60640-4710
Phone: (312)878-0681
Fax: (312)878-0682

"The Law is the Weapon; the Courtroom the Battlefield, the Judge is your Enemy, your Lawyer is an Enemy Spy."

Ask for the free "Info-Pak" containing numerous useful tools & services for lawyerless litigators. Offers books such as *The Irwin Rommel School of Law: How to Defeat an Illegal Legal System*, By Michael H. Brown among others, as well as audio and video tapes, seminars, sample pleadings, and legal research services.

**Please mention that you were referred by information in this book.

VOCAL (Victims of Child Abuse Laws)
There are local chapters of VOCAL nationwide. Your best bet is to contact the chapter nearest you.
National Association of State VOCAL Chapters (NASVO/VOCAL) Internet address - www.vocal.org
I would also suggest doing a web search for [victims of child abuse laws]

> "Founded February 28, 1987. In that the family is the cradle of human society, rich and diverse with religion, ethnicity, custom, and culture; and that from the family comes the child, within and through whom lies the future of that society; it is vital that we move towards empowering the family, be developing resources that nurture, educate and protect; and in doing so, prevent unnecessary and arbitrary government interference, and promote equity and justice under the law."
>
> VOCAL is a support group for people who have been falsely accused of child abuse. They have lists of experienced lawyers, reference materials, conferences, tapes and videos, and in many cases a newsletter.

Right Way l.a.w. (learn and win)
c/o 3463 Massillon Road Suite 363
Uniontown, Ohio state
NonDomestic 44685
Phone: (330)699-1605
Fax: (330)699-1656
NOTE: when you call for information please say you were referred by member #2726
Internet address - http://www.netonecom.net/~gwood/

> "Right Way l.a.w. is a voluntary unincorporated association. The Club's primary objective is to share legal knowledge and to educate members to

understand and use the legal system in a lawful manner."

American De Jure Alliance
2313 Lockhill-Selma Road
Suite 241
San Antonio, Texas 78230
Internet address - http://www.adja.com

"The American De Jure Alliance was founded in April of 1996 out of the desire to see a de jure government return to the united States of America. The ADJA is a network of dedicated individuals from around the country who are experts in their respective fields. The ongoing mission of the ADJA is the research, coordination, and dissemination of information on the law and legal processes."

Home School Legal Defense Association
Part of the National Center for Home Education
PO Box 125
Paeonian Springs, VA 22129
Phone: (703)338-7600
Internet Address -
(http://www.learnathome.com/hslda.htm

"Each year home schooling families across America receive unfriendly legal contacts from government officials [including a large number of false allegations of child abuse]. Whether those contacts lead to court or not, families who fight their legal battles alone face the threat of staggering legal expenses mostly for attorneys' fees. Rather than pay the price of resisting, many families are intimidated into abandoning home schooling. The purpose of the Home School Legal Defense Association is to bring together a large number of home schooling families so that each can have a low-cost method of obtaining quality legal defense. We give families the freedom to home school without the fear of facing legal threats alone."

Author' note: While I received valuable legal infromation from this organization, I am greatly disturbed by some of the views and political positions of the head of the HSLDA, Michael Farris. I have heard numerous bad things about him from various, unrelated sources, among these: He appears to be an advocate of the Parental Rights and Responsibilities Act which actually gives the government more control over your children. He also appears to advocate a Constitutional Convention, a dangerous concept because it could utterly destroy our current constitution. Despite what proponents say, nothing is out of bounds during a Con-Con. Are righteous home-schoolers paying for their own demise? If this is true, perhaps home-schoolers need to cancel their membership with this organization and form another one that isn't intent upon violating our few remaining rights, or put pressure on the organization to discard Michael Farris. If this concerns you, I suggest you look into it and make your own decision.

BIBLIOGRAPHY

Kauser, Janson A. *The Social Services Gestapo*. Lafayatte, LA: Huntington House Publishers, 1995

Guzman, Ingrid J. *Parent Police*. Lafayatte, LA: Huntington House Publishers, 1995

Scott, Brenda. *Out of Control.* Lafayatte, LA: Huntington House Publishers, 1995

Georges, Jeannie. *Outcome Based Education.* Evansville, IN: TreeTop Communications, Inc., 1995
Media Bypass Magazine, PO Box 5326, Evansville, IN 47716. (812)477-8670

Hearn, Donna. *Paychecks and Power.* The Constitutional Coalition, 1995
PO Box 37054, St. Louis, MO 37054

Simonds, Kathi. *A Critique of America 200, An Education Strategy*. Citizens for Excellence in Education, 1991. PO Box 3200, Costa Mesa, CA 82628

Eakman, B. K. *Educating for the 'New World Order'.* Portland, OR: Halcyon House, 1991.

Colorado Children's Trust Fund. *Re-Visioning a Future for Colorado's Children and Youth.* Colorado Children's Trust Fund Department of Social Work, 1995.

Colorado Children's Trust Fund. *Child Maltreatment in Colorado: The Value of Prevention and the Cost of Failure to Prevent.* Colorado Children's Trust Fund Department of Social Work, 1995.

Delaplane, David and Anne. *Victims: A Manual for Clergy and Congregations.* Fourth Edition. The Spiritual Dimension in Victim Services, PO Box 6736, Denver, CO 80206.

Hart, Kimberly A. *Guilty Until Proven Innocent: A Manual for Surviving False Allegations of Child Abuse.* Kimberly A. Hart, National Child Abuse Defense & Resource Center, Inc., 1989.

Ceci, Stephen J. (Cornell University) and Bruck, Maggie (McGill University). *The Suggestibility of the Child Witness: A Historical Review and Synthesis.* Revised May 18, 1992. S.J. Ceci, Department of Human Development, Cornell University, Ithica, NY 14853.

Schuman, Daniel C. M.D. *False Accusations of Physical and Sexual Abuse.* Director of Psychiatry, Norfolk County Probate and Family Court; Assistant Clinical Professor of Psychiatry, Tufts Medical School. 1984.

Symposium: *Licensing Parents.* Society, November/December 1996.

My two favorite books on discipline:

Dobson, James C. *Dare to Discipline.* Wheaton, IL; Tyndale House Publishers, 1978

Dobson, James C. *The Strong Willed Child: Birth to Adolesence.* Wheaton, IL; Tyndale House Publishers, 1970.